◄SPEAR

1ST MARINE DIVISION
IN VIETNAM

First to Fight

We fight our country's battles
In the air, on land, and sea.
First to fight for right and freedom,
And to keep our honor clean,
We are proud to claim the title
Of United States Marines.

SPEARHEAD

1st Marine Division
In Vietnam

Simon Dunstan

ZENITH PRESS

First published in 2008 by Zenith Press, an imprint of MBI Publishing Company, 400 1st Avenue North, Minneapolis, MN 55401 USA.

Zenith Press titles are also available at discounts in bulk quantity for industrial or sales-promotional use. For details write to Special Sales Manager at MBI Publishing Company, 400 1st Avenue North, Minneapolis, MN 55401 USA.

To find out more about our books, join us online at www.zenithpress.com.

ISBN-13: 978-0-7603-3159-0

Design: Compendium Design
Layout and editorial: Donald Sommerville
Maps: Mark Franklin

Printed in Singapore

Note: Internet site information provided in the Reference section was correct when provided by the author. The publisher can accept no responsibility for this information becoming incorrect.

Unless otherwise noted, all the photographs in this book are reproduced courtesy of the National Archives and Records Administration at College Park, Maryland or the U.S. Marine Corps History Division. The author would like to extend his thanks to Kevin Lyles and Steven Zaloga for their unstinting assistance in the preparation of this book as well as those Marines who provided their recollections. As always, the U.S. Marine Corps History Division provided invaluable information and research material.

CONTENTS

THE OLD BREED

Between 1961 and 1973, a total of 47,244 U.S. service personnel were killed and 303,704 wounded by direct enemy action in Vietnam.

Marine Corps Strength	
30 June 1918	52,819
30 June 1939	19,432
31 May 1945	471,369
30 April 1952	242,017
30 June 1968	307,252
31 December 1976	188,506
31 December 1997	159,100
2008	188,000

The 1st Marine Division is one of the most distinguished military formations in the U.S. armed forces. The division was formally activated on board the battleship USS *Texas* on 1 February 1941 but its constituent units can trace their lineage back over many years and numerous wars around the world. Originally organized as the Continental Marines on 10 November 1775 as naval infantry, the Marine Corps has served in every American armed conflict including the Revolutionary War. The fighting formations of the division comprised, and do so to this day, three infantry regiments, the 1st, 5th, and 7th, and an artillery regiment, the 11th, together with supporting arms. This was the first actual division in U.S. Marine Corps (USMC) history. The primary role of the division was and remains amphibious assault from the sea as a projection of American power around the world.

The 1st Marine Infantry Regiment, but known simply as the 1st Marines, was formed at Guantanamo Bay on the Caribbean island of Cuba on 8 March 1911—54 years to the day before Marine troops landed on the beaches of South Vietnam at the outset of the longest war fought by the Marine Corps. The regiment saw action on Haiti in 1915 and in the Dominican Republic during 1916—familiar stamping grounds for the Marines for much of the 20th century—with the protection of the Panama Canal as the primary strategic imperative. The 5th Marines followed on 13 July 1914 at Vera Cruz in Mexico. The regiment fought on the Western Front during the Great War at such decisive battles as Belleau Wood, Château Thierry, and St Mihiel—all being subsequently commemorated in the names of U.S. Navy troop-ships, aircraft carriers or assault landing ships. The 7th Marines was formed on 7 August 1917 at Philadelphia and served in Cuba for the remainder of the war. These three Marine infantry regiments have formed the backbone of the division throughout its combat history.

The principal fire-support element of the division is the 11th Marines. It was originally activated as a light artillery regiment on 3 January 1918 at Marine Barracks at Quantico, Virginia—the home of

German trench mortar captured by 2nd Battalion, 5th Marines, at Belleau Wood. Marine legend states that following this decisive clash the German defenders gave their U.S. attackers the nickname of *Teufelshunde* or "Devil Dogs" for their ferocity in battle, a term that Marines exalt to this day in many forms from personal tattoos to recruiting posters. The "Devil Dogs" are justly proud of this action, for although it is sometimes seen as "an inconsequential affair" against the bigger canvas of World War I, more USMC troops fell in the attack on Belleau Wood than had died in combat in the whole of the unit's history up till then. The final cost was around half the Marine force. The action had stopped the German attack towards Paris and, quite possibly, saved the day for the Allies. In recognition of their prowess the wood was renamed Bois de la Brigade de Marine. *TRH Pictures*

the Marine Corps. However, the men trained as infantry to act as reinforcements for the Western Front but arrived in France too late to see action. Following the war the regiment was decommissioned on 11 August 1919 but reactivated on 9 May 1927 to fight insurgents, train militia forces—the Guardia Nacional—and supervise elections in Nicaragua in 1928, tasks so redolent of subsequent wars in Vietnam and Iraq. On 31 August 1929, the 11th Marines was disbanded once again before being re-formed as a fully-fledged artillery unit on 1 March 1940 at Guantanamo Bay to become the integral artillery regiment of the 1st Marine Division, a role it continues to execute to this day. Other Marine combat support elements followed, such as the 1st Marine Aircraft Wing on 7 July 1941 and the 1st Tank Battalion on 1 November 1941.

Throughout these formative years, the Marine Corps pursued its primary role as the amphibious assault force of the U.S. Navy to which it was attached. Exercises large and small were conducted at Quantico and at New River, North Carolina, later to become Camp Lejeune, to formulate a comprehensive doctrine for amphibious operations. Fundamental to this was the means to transport troops from ships to shore in sufficient numbers and with adequate protection to fulfil the military purpose of the operation, particularly against a contested beachhead. Prior to Pearl Harbor, there was a paucity of effective landing craft; ship-to-shore communications were rudimentary; and coordinated fire control of naval gunfire and the close air support of the 1st Marine Aircraft Wing was still in its infancy.

Innovative designers such as Andrew J. Higgins and Donald Roebling Jr. rose to the challenge. Higgins, a New Orleans boat builder, constructed shallow-draft Eureka support craft for offshore oilrigs drilling in the Gulf of Mexico. At his own expense, he modified a Eureka boat with a retractable bow ramp based on a design suggested by Capt. Victor H. Krulak who, as a young officer with the 4th Marines in Shanghai in 1937, had observed Japanese assault boats in action. This modified Eureka became the forerunner of the LCVP, Landing Craft Vehicles and Personnel, and a host of other landing craft of World War 2 that were fundamental to victory in the Pacific campaigns. General Krulak later became the Commanding General, Fleet Marine Force, Pacific, and overall commander of Marine formations in Vietnam from 1964 until 1968.

Equally important was the amphibian tractor to transport troops to the shoreline together with their combat supplies. The grandson of the builder of the Brooklyn Bridge, Donald Roebling, developed a rescue vehicle capable of operating on both land and water in the state of Florida following a hurricane in the region in 1928. The first experimental vehicle appeared in 1937 with the name of Alligator. It attracted the attention of the Marine Corps after an article appeared in

U.S. Marine Corps LVT-1 amphibian tractors churn towards the beaches of Guadacanal during the landings of August 1942 – the first time the LVT was used in combat. At this time the Alligators of the 1st and 2nd Amphibian Tractor Battalions were used to provide logistical support to bring supplies ashore rather than as troop carriers in the assault. The latter role was first demonstrated against the Japanese island fortress of Betio in the Tarawa atoll in November 1943.

Life magazine in the 4 October 1937 issue. A trials vehicle was purchased by the USMC in November 1940 and an order for 200 was awarded to Roebling in February 1941. Unable to fulfil such a large contract, Roebling passed the manufacture of the LVT, or Landing Vehicle Tracked, to the Food Machinery Corporation at Dunedin, Florida. Later famous as the producers of the M113 APC series, FMC completed the first two Alligators in July. The LVT became the standard equipment for the 1st Amphibian Tractor Battalion that became part of the 1st Marine Division in February 1942, although at this stage the "amtracs," as they were generically known from the term "amphibian tractor," were only intended as amphibious resupply vehicles. In the words of General Holland "Howling Mad" Smith USMC: "The development of the amphibian tractor, or LVT, which began in the middle 1930s, provided the solution and was one of the most important modern technical contributions to ship-to-shore operations. Without these landing vehicles our amphibious offensive in the Pacific would have been impossible."

All the elements were now in place for the 1st Marine Division to undertake the daunting task of assaulting the many heavily defended islands held by the Japanese imperial forces across the thousands of hostile miles of the western Pacific Ocean. On 7 August 1942, the division attacked the islands of Guadalcanal and Tulagi in a ferocious six-month struggle that resulted in over 3,000 Marine casualties. Guadacanal became the division's primary battle honor and is emblazoned on its insignia. After a period of rest and recuperation in Australia, the division returned to combat in late 1943 in New Guinea and New Britain. On 15 September 1944, three amtrac battalions spearheaded the assault landing on Peleliu in the Caroline Islands supported by M4 Sherman tanks of the 1st Tank Battalion. Again Marine casualties were staggering in number as the tenacious Japanese garrison fought to the last. Peleliu was followed by Okinawa which proved to be the longest and deadliest campaign of the Pacific war. Following the Japanese surrender, the 1st Marine Division was deployed on occupation duties in northern China where further casualties were incurred in clashes with the Chinese communists in a bitter foretaste of the conflict to come.

The gun crew of an M1A1 75mm Pack Howitzer on Carriage M8 prepare to fire their weapon from a captured Japanese emplacement during the fighting on the island of Tulagi in August 1942 as part of the major Marine operation in support of the landings on Guadacanal. In ferocious fighting the Japanese garrison on Tulagi was slaughtered almost to the last man. As of April 1943, USMC divisional artillery included three 75mm howitzer battalions, each of 12 pieces. On account of its low weight of 1,436 pounds, the pack howitzer (later designated M116) was relatively easy to maneuver in the difficult terrain of the Pacific atolls and islands and was a crucial fire support weapon to the Marine riflemen in combat.

By the end of World War 2, the U.S. Marine Corps was the true exemplar of amphibious warfare, but the price of victory had been high. The Marine Corps suffered 91,718 casualties with 19,733 killed and missing, together with 71,985 wounded on active service. Despite rapid post-war demobilization, a deep well of expertise remained in the Marine Corps and it was soon put to the test once more when communist North Korea invaded its southern neighbor in June 1950.

Exhausted riflemen of 2/7 Marines clamber aboard LVT-3C amtracs of the 1st Amphibious Tractor Battalion at Hungnam harbor on 11 December 1950 for redeployment after their epic 13-day fighting withdrawal from the Chosin Reservoir following the intervention of Chinese Communist Forces in the Korean War.

Within weeks, the Republic of Korea Army was forced back to a shrinking perimeter around the southern port of Pusan, together with the remnants of U.S. Army troops rushed to the frontlines from occupation duties in Japan while reinforcements were deployed from the United States. Despite the desperate overall situation, General Douglas MacArthur, head of the United Nations Command Korea, instructed the Marine Corps to prepare for an amphibious assault landing far behind enemy lines in an ambitious counteroffensive. With the 5th Marines fighting with the Marine Provisional Brigade to stabilize the Pusan Perimeter, the remainder of the 1st Marine Division set sail from California in August.

The assault landing at the port of Inchon, near the South Korean capital of Seoul, on 15 September 1950 was arguably the most brilliant operation in the annals of amphibious warfare since Wolfe captured the Heights of Abraham. Facing one of the most extreme tidal flows in the world, the landing ships had but a short space of time to deposit the troops before they were completely cut off from any reinforcements until the next high tide. Nevertheless, the landings were a spectacular success and Seoul was soon recaptured. The bulk of the North Korean Army was now trapped and at the mercy of U.S. airpower. There followed the invasion of North Korea, but this precipitated open conflict with the sleeping giant—China. The result was a debacle for American arms but the 1st Marine Division won immortal fame at the battle of the Chosin Reservoir in November. In the most atrocious weather conditions, the division broke out of an enemy encirclement and made an orderly fighting withdrawal to Hungnam with most of its men and equipment, while inflicting horrendous casualties on the Chinese forces. After months of bitter fighting, the frontlines became virtually static along the 38th Parallel that had been the pre-war border.

For the next two years of hostilities, the 1st Marine Division was essentially employed as just another infantry formation, a role far removed from the audacious assault on Inchon. To add insult to injury, the division remained in Korea until March 1955 with a further wasting of its principal expertise in amphibious warfare. Marine Corps casualties during the war were 30,544, including 4,506 dead and missing and 26,038 wounded.

Despite the lack of amphibious operations in the static phase of the Korean War, the U.S. Marine Corps set itself at the forefront of technological and tactical innovation with the first widespread use of helicopters in combat. This included the concept of "vertical envelopment" to insert fully armed troops on to the battlefield—although the helicopters of the day were badly constrained by low lift capabilities and the high altitudes in the mountainous Korean terrain. Over the coming years, the Marine Corps refined its doctrine of helicopter assault operations. When the call came to engage in another Asian conflict, Marine aviators were ready to respond. On Palm Sunday, 15 April 1962, Marine Medium Helicopter Squadron 362 (HMM-362) was established at an abandoned Japanese airstrip at Soc Trang in the Mekong Delta in an area dominated by the insurgent forces known as the Viet Cong (or VC) and just 85 miles from the South Vietnamese capital of Saigon.

Crewmen of Company A, 1st Marine Tank Battalion, load their M26 Pershings with 90-mm ammunition rounds on board a landing craft prior to the amphibious assault against the port of Inchon, Korea, 15 September 1950.

IN ACTION

Like Korea, Vietnam had been artificially divided in two with the communists in the North and the Republic of Vietnam in the south. By the brutal logic of the Cold War, the United States supported the autocratic and corrupt regime of South Vietnam against the Viet Cong insurgency backed by the communist North that in turn was supported by China and the Soviet Union. Marine Corps advisors had been present in South Vietnam since the departure of the French in 1954 to train Vietnamese forces but HMM-362 was the first Marine unit to see action in the far distant country of South Vietnam. It was the first of many in the longest and bitterest war fought by the U.S. Marine Corps and the 1st Marine Division, culminating in the aerial evacuation of personnel from the roof of the U.S. Embassy in Saigon in April 1975 by the Marine helicopters of HMM-164.

In the early years of the Vietnam War, the UH-34D Choctaw was the standard medium helicopter in service with the U.S. Marine Corps. This type, originally designated Sikorsky HUS-1, was first used in South Vietnam by HMM-362 from April 1962 as part of Operation Shufly to provide the ARVN forces with greater mobility and logistical support against the elusive insurgent enemy in the Mekong Delta region. The arrival of U.S. Marine Corps and U.S. Army helicopters in South Vietnam during 1962 came as a rude shock to Hanoi. In 1960, Ho Chi Minh declared that victory in the South would be achieved within the year. In 1962, with the increasing use of helicopters and U.S. airpower, he revised his prediction to 15 years. He was almost right.

The Da Nang Landings

The UH-34 helicopters of HMM-362 and succeeding squadrons provided much needed mobility to the overstretched units of the Army of the Republic of Vietnam (ARVN) against the elusive Viet Cong. In

Terrain was a constant constraint on the effectiveness of American maneuver battalions in the field. Cruelly burdened with equipment and weapons weighing anything up to 80 pounds, it was not feasible for US troops to match the mobility of the enemy on the ground. Eschewing any form of body armor or even combat boots when flip-flops would suffice, an NVA/Viet Cong soldier commonly carried less than half the load of his American counterpart. Coupled with his intimate knowledge of the terrain over which he travelled or fought, he invariably enjoyed greater freedom of movement at night and rarely sought combat except when at a distinct tactical advantage. However, once battle was joined, the NVA/VC often displayed a lack of flexibility, particularly in set-piece actions such as the assault of a fire support base.

September 1962, HMM-163 moved from Soc Trang to the airbase at Da Nang, some 380 miles north of Saigon, and close to the Demilitarized Zone (or DMZ) that marked the border between North and South Vietnam. Over the next two years the political and military situation in Vietnam deteriorated markedly while American casualties rose steadily. The principal American military support came from helicopter units to provide ARVN troops with increased mobility and attack aircraft for their fire support. Aircraft also conducted air strikes against North Vietnam. Many of these came from aircraft carriers of the U.S. Seventh Fleet sailing off the coast of Vietnam and increasingly from airbases on land such as Da Nang, Bien Hoa, and Tan Son Nhut. As these bases grew in size and importance, they became ready targets

A World War 2 artilleryman, Superintendent of West Point and former commander of the 101st Airborne Division, General William Childs Westmorland took over Military Assistance Command Vietnam in August 1964. From the outset, he and MACV were at odds with III MAF and Marine commanders over the conduct of the war. This came to a head over the deployment of Marines to an abandoned hilltop camp known as Khe Sanh, a location that the Marines discounted as irrelevant. After the Tet Offensive, mutual trust was irrevocably damaged and was not restored until all the principal commanders were replaced.

OPPOSITE: South Vietnam was divided into four Military Regions or Corps Tactical Zones, each with distinctly different terrain features.

for Viet Cong rocket and ground attacks. Accordingly, ground troops were required to ensure their protection and at Da Nang that meant the Marines.

In the morning of 8 March 1965, the 3rd Battalion, 9th Marines, of the 3rd Marine Division's 9th Marine Expeditionary Brigade came ashore in an unopposed landing on Red Beach 2, northwest of Da Nang—the first American ground infantry troops to serve in South Vietnam. Unlike in most landings conducted by the Marine Corps, they were greeted by a brass band and Vietnamese women dispensing flower garlands. After securing the perimeter at the airbase, the men of 3/9 watched U.S. Air Force (USAF) C-130 Hercules aircraft land to disembark the 1st Battalion, 9th Marines. Back in the U.S.A. the event hardly made the news as Dr Martin Luther King's Civil Rights march from Selma to Montgomery was dominating the headlines. It was the beginning of the massive troop build-up in South Vietnam that was to cost the lives of over 58,000 Americans and many billions of dollars of national treasure. And for years it was hardly ever out of the news.

During the following months, more Marine formations were deployed to South Vietnam, including Marine fixed-wing assets such as the F-4B Phantom II fighter bombers of VMFA-531. By May, the 3rd Marine Division was almost complete in-country. The 9th Marine Expeditionary Brigade was redesignated as III Marine Amphibious Force or III MAF to embrace the 3rd Marine Division and the 1st Marine Aircraft Wing as well as support elements. The term "Amphibious" was preferred to "Expeditionary" as the latter smacked of the colonialist French Expeditionary Corps of the 1950s. Under the command of Maj. Gen. Lewis W. Walt, III MAF soon wished to expand its Tactical Area of Responsibility (TAOR) to eliminate the "rocket belt" around its airbases within I Corps Tactical Zone (I CTZ).

South Vietnam was divided into four Military Regions or Corps Tactical Zones with I CTZ comprising the five northern provinces of South Vietnam. Throughout the war, I CTZ, or "Eye Core" as it was called by Marines, was their major area of operations with the 3rd Marine Division in the two northernmost provinces adjoining the DMZ (Quang Tri and Thua Thinh) and the 1st Marine Division mostly in the three provinces to the south (Quang Nam, Quang Tin, and Quang Ngai). By now there were 51,000 U.S. servicemen in South Vietnam, including 16,500 Marines, under the overall command of U.S. Army General William C. Westmoreland. From the outset, there was a difference of opinion between the Military Assistance Command Vietnam (MACV) in Saigon and the Marine Corps as to how to conduct the war, let alone between the in-country military leaders and the politicians in Washington, DC. With their long experience of "small wars," the Marines realized immediately that this was a

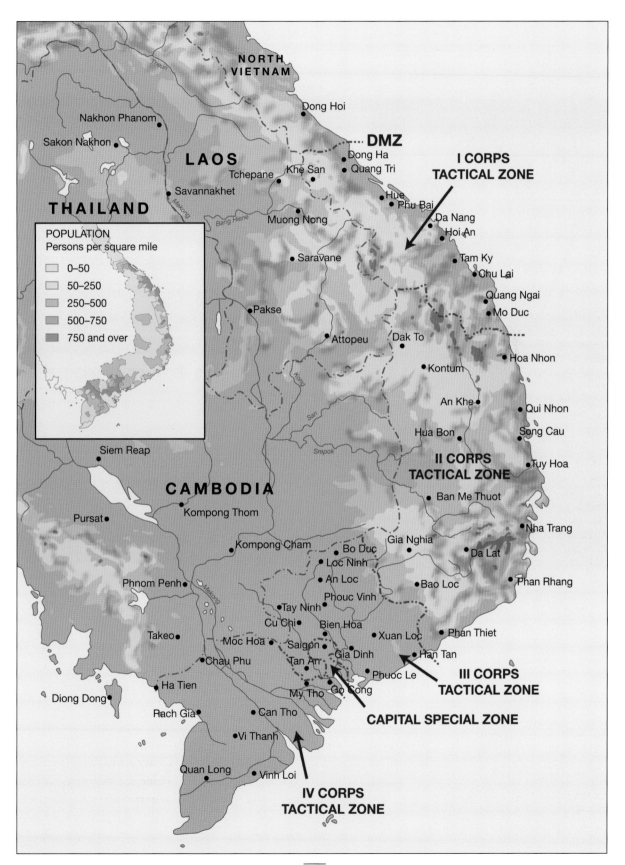

NORTH
VIETNAM

Dong Hoi

DMZ

**I CORPS
TACTICAL ZONE**

Nakhon Phanom

Sakon Nakhon

LAOS

Tchepane   Khe San   Dong Ha
                          Quang Tri

Savannakhet

THAILAND

Muong Nong

Hue
Phu Bai

Da Nang
Hoi An

Saravane

Tam Ky
Chu Lai

POPULATION
Persons per square mile

0–50
50–250
250–500
500–750
750 and over

Pakse

Attopeu   Dak To

Quang Ngai
Mo Duc

Hoa Nhon

Kontum

An Khe

Qui Nhon

Song Cau

Hua Bon

Siem Reap

**II CORPS
TACTICAL ZONE**

Tuy Hoa

CAMBODIA

Ban Me Thuot

Kompong Thom

Nha Trang

Pursat

Gia Nghia

Kompong Cham   Bo Duc
                 Loc Ninh
Phnom Penh   An Loc
                 Phouc Vinh

Da Lat

Bao Loc

Phan Rhang

Tay Ninh
Cu Chi   Bien Hoa

Takeo   Moc Hoa

Xuan Loc   Phan Thiet

Chau Phu   Saigon   Gia Dinh   Han Tan
             Tan An
                        Phuoc Le   **III CORPS
                                     TACTICAL ZONE**

Ha Tien   My Tho   Go Cong

Diong Dong

CAPITAL SPECIAL ZONE

Rach Gia   Can Tho

Vi Thanh

Quan Long   Vinh Loi

**IV CORPS
TACTICAL ZONE**

One of the overreaching problems in Vietnam was to identify enemy insurgents among the civilian population and this was never resolved throughout the duration of the conflict as shown with young males of military age being led away as prisoners to be processed by South Vietnamese government officials.

counterinsurgency campaign that to succeed required the cooperation of the Vietnamese people—"winning the hearts and minds"—through the protection of their villages and livelihoods. Only then could Allied forces, both ARVN and Marine, expand their military operations outwards from the coastal enclaves, where the vast majority of the civilian population lived, to engage and destroy the main-force Viet Cong units hiding in the hinterland. Together with construction and education projects to aid the local people, this was known as the "inkblot strategy" as advocated by the Marines. It was exemplified by the Combined Action Program or CAP as originally undertaken by small teams of Marines throughout their TAORs as a primary mission of "pacification" rather than warfighting.

General Westmoreland had very different ideas. Under growing political pressure from Washington for immediate success on the battlefield, he was obliged to seek out and destroy the elusive enemy wherever they could be found, fixed in place, and then wiped out. This proved to be nigh-on impossible while South Vietnamese communist insurgents were able to blend in with the local population—the proverbial farmer by day and fighter by night—and North Vietnamese army regulars were able to hide completely in the rugged mountainous terrain and jungles, or when threatened to withdraw to comfortable sanctuaries in neighboring "neutral" Cambodia and Laos. From these hidden bases, the enemy were able to mount operations at a time and a place of their own choosing and avoid contact whenever the opposition seemed too strong. Over 80 percent of combat contacts during the Vietnam War were initiated by the Viet Cong or North Vietnamese. American and allied forces could only react; and more often than not when they were ambushed the tactical advantage lay with the enemy. It was a fundamental problem that was never resolved during the war.

Costly operations in the border regions such as the battle of the Ia Drang Valley conducted by the U.S. Army 1st Cavalry Division (Airmobile) in November 1965 did little to protect or secure the 80 percent of the population that lived along the coastal belt of South Vietnam in just 10 percent of the country's landmass. In reality, Westmoreland did not have sufficient troops to conduct either the strategy of pursuing the main-force enemy to destruction or the pacification of the countryside to protect the people. For every rifleman Westmoreland gained grudgingly from Washington, Hanoi was able to provide two or more to support its aim to unite North and South Vietnam by force. It was all the more tragic then that Westmoreland decided to pursue a policy of attrition to fight the war through "search and destroy" operations. When asked how he was to achieve his given war aim his answer was simply "firepower." Despite their deep misgivings the high command of III MAF had no choice but to obey their overall commander in-country.

The NVA and Viet Cong proved to be formidable enemies during the Vietnam War. All of them were able to endure the most severe hardships yet still remain militarily effective. With only the most rudimentary medical services and logistical support, they displayed a remarkable level of strategic and tactical mobility even under overwhelming US air supremacy and firepower. Despite the fame and reputation of the AK47, the standard infantry weapon was the 7.62-mm SKS semi-automatic rifle as shown here with a folding bayonet. Unlike his American rival, the NVA/VC soldier tended to travel light to increase mobility and aid concealment. Commonly referred to as Victor Charlie from the radio phonetic alphabet for VC, Marines also called him "Mr Charles" as a sign of respect; similarly his NVA partner was known as "Mr Nguyen." Veteran Marine Combat Correspondent Keyes Beech summed up the enemy with the words "I would like to offer a salute to that skinny little Viet Cong somewhere out there in the jungle shivering in the monsoon rains . . . he is one hell of a fighting man."

Arrival of 1st Marine Division

Never let it be said that the Marines were unwilling to expand their area of operations and engage the enemy in battle. Yet to their credit they never forsook their pacification programs either and many of them met with quiet success—the true measure of a well-conducted counter-insurgency campaign. Nevertheless, with more Marine units arriving in-country, including some from the 1st Marine Division, III MAF began planning offensive operations. By 6 July 1965, all the units of the 3rd Marine Division were deployed in South Vietnam. On the following day, the 2nd Battalion, 7th Marines became the first unit of the 1st Marine Division to be fully committed to the Vietnam War when it landed at Qui Nhon in II CTZ to protect the expanding U.S. Army logistical base there. In August, the 1st Marines began deployment from California with the 1st Battalion arriving at Da Nang on the 25th. The other battalions and the regimental headquarters followed and were all in-country by January 1966 under the operational command of the 3rd Marine Division before reverting to the 1st Marine Division on 28 March 1966.

On 18 August 1965, the Marines launched their first major offensive of the war with Operation Starlite against the 1st Viet Cong Regiment that was preparing to attack the airstrip at Chu Lai. In a concerted

Sheltering behind the paddy dikes, men of 2nd Platoon, Mike Company, 3/7 Marines, regroup after a firefight with the Viet Cong during Operation Jackson in Quang Nai Province on 29 August 1966. Steam fills the air as the assistant gunner of an M60 team uses his M1 helmet to pour rice paddy water over the red-hot barrel of the machine gun This illustrates one of the problems of the M60—after sustained firing the barrel tended to overheat, often necessitating a change of barrel. However, because the barrel had no handle, the assistant gunner was provided with a large asbestos mitten but this was rarely carried in the field because of its bulk. Hence other measures had to be taken to cool down the weapon.

combined-arms operation embracing the insertion of troops by helicopters and from the sea, supported by artillery, naval gunfire, tanks, and LVTP-5 amtracs, 614 Viet Cong were killed and nine captured as well as 109 weapons in a week-long encounter at a cost of 45 Marines dead and 203 wounded. Already the gruesome mathematics of the "body count" had begun to appear in after-action reports. The operation was controlled by Headquarters, 7th Marines, with 3/7 Marines in reserve but committed to battle together with the artillery support of 3rd Battalion, 11th Marines, and Battery M, 4/11. These units, together with 1/7, conducted a follow-up operation codenamed Piranha against the battered 1st Viet Cong Regiment that had retreated to the Batangan Peninsula.

On this occasion, under the specific instructions of General Westmoreland, the ARVN was part of the planning process for Operation Piranha since its generals had taken offense at being excluded from Operation Starlite. Operation Piranha began on 7 September with an assault landing by the amtracs of 3rd Amphibian Tractor Battalion carrying 1/7 Marines, followed by an air assault with UH-34s transporting 3/7 and then two ARVN battalions. Enemy resistance was minimal and with good reason—the 1st Viet Cong Regiment had fled several days before. The only significant contact of the operation occurred when Company B, 1/7, came across a VC field hospital in a cave complex. When called upon to surrender the VC refused so, in an episode harking back to Okinawa and a score of battles in the Pacific, Marine engineers detonated an explosive charge in the cave killing 66 VC. Overall casualties for the operation were 178 VC dead as against 2 Marines and 5 ARVN killed with a further 14 Marines and 33 Vietnamese wounded.

Operations Starlite and Piranha were an early microcosm of the Vietnam War and indicative of the problems facing allied forces in any military operation to defend the Republic of Vietnam. During Starlite the Marines were able to pin the enemy with their backs to the sea where they were subjected to devastating firepower but even so many escaped. This, however, was based on good intelligence and the circumstances of topography plus the essential operational security that was only achieved by excluding the ARVN from the operation. In Operation Piranha, operational security was compromised and the enemy fled without significant contact while supporting fire was constrained against fleeting targets for fear of hitting civilian non-combatants. Therein lay the dilemma. Operations were only really successful if based on valid and timely intelligence and this often came from the ARVN but the latter was also a major source of information to the enemy. Furthermore, if firepower was the principal means to win battles, then any collateral damage risked alienating the very people that the war was being fought to protect.

Lance Cpl. Spees gives a member of the Vietnamese Marine Corps instruction in the use of an M18 APERS Claymore anti-personnel mine; he is inserting the M57 electrical firing device into the weapon and ensuring the mine is properly orientated; to this end the mine is inscribed in large letters— FRONT TOWARD ENEMY. Note the Vietnamese Marine is wearing the distinctive Marine Corps utility cap known universally as a "cover." The first U.S. Marine Corps advisor to serve in South Vietnam was Captain Victor J. Croizat, a specialist in amphibious warfare; he arrived in 1954 to help the ARVN create a Vietnamese Marine Corps.

Yet, if the war was to be won, it was incumbent upon the ARVN to conduct military and civic operations in a committed and professional manner to defend their own country, but this was barely feasible given the nature of South Vietnamese society. Many ARVN officers were highly competent, having pursued the profession of arms since the First Indochina War, but they were saddled with reluctant conscripts required to fight for a corrupt regime without respite and often without pay. There was no 365-day tour of duty for the ARVN soldier and his first instinct was survival by avoiding any fighting if at all possible. In the higher echelons of the officer corps, many appointments were based on loyalty to the hierarchy in Saigon and loyalty was bought by corruption involving all manner of criminality from smuggling and extortion to embezzlement of soldiers' pay. There were exceptions such as the General Reserve comprising the Vietnamese Marine Corps and ARVN airborne forces but these were not configured for counter-insurgency operations and could always be marginalized if need be; in general these units were based far from Saigon so they could not readily be employed for a *coup d'état*. In reality the war was a hopeless cause even from these earliest days.

Into this maelstrom of deceit, intrigue, and corruption were thrown the young American soldiers and Marines, volunteers and draftees, drawn from every state of the Union to fight in a country very few had even heard of, for a cause few could understand beyond the clarion call of fighting communism in all its manifestations. They landed in a country and a culture that were totally alien and among a people who affected studied indifference and with whom communication was impractical. Laden down with heavy weapons and uncomfortable body armor in the stultifying heat or enervating rain, the Marines were

Tour of Duty

During the Vietnam War, officers served for only six months in combat commands. This policy arose because the Pentagon believed that the war would be of short duration and this would allow the maximum number of officers to experience command in the field in order to enhance their career progression. When it was realized that the war would not be short-lived, the policy continued on the spurious basis that a six-month tour of duty would reduce the likelihood of exhaustion or burnout, a notion that amused many ARVN officers who had been fighting the Viet Minh/Viet Cong for ten years or more. This misguided policy was immensely disruptive to unit cohesion as junior officers came and went with depressing regularity due to serial rotation, failure, or as casualties—officers and their radiomen were prime targets for snipers. Young and inexperienced in the skills of bushcraft, a new officer had but a short time to impress his superiors, so action spoke louder than words. Action meant fulfilling the body count quota by finding an enemy who largely only fought on his own terms. This led to unnecessary friendly casualties, often due to the officer's rashness, inexperience, or desire to emulate Marine Corps heroes of the past. Such actions were unlikely to endear a new "butterbar" to his enlisted men, much less an anonymous major or "bird" colonel. Due to the increasingly technical nature of modern warfare there was also a significant expansion of the officer corps with 16 percent (1 officer to 6 men) during the Vietnam War as against 6 percent in Korea (1 to 15). In time this led to too many officers chasing too few commands, which further increased the pressures for immediate results at a time that the soldiers' morale was flagging.

In the U.S. Army, a soldier served for one year in South Vietnam—the fabled "365 Days." In the Marine Corps, a tour of duty lasted for 13 months—traditionally because of the extra time a Marine spent at sea going to and from the battle zone but hardly fair in the era of jet airliners.

For the first six weeks or so an FNG (f***ing new guy) was as green as a banana leaf and as much a danger to himself and his comrades as he was to the enemy. During this period a novice rifleman was most likely to become a casualty. Once he had learned the ropes the hard way, he was accepted into the squad and even given a name. He then honed his new-found skills—if he was big and strong, as an M60 gunner or, if he had the knack, as the

With his M14 rifle slung across his shoulder, 2nd Lt. Jim Kyle confers with ARVN soldiers during an operation in Quang Nam Province in June 1970. Under their identical M1 helmets, the disparity in sizes between the Vietnamese and the American is graphically illustrated. Kyle is wearing the Marine Corps M1955 fragmentation vest with a rope ridge on the shoulder to prevent the rifle butt from slipping on the waterproof ballistic nylon covering of the body armor. This is the later version of the flak vest introduced in late 1967 with a webbing strip around the bottom edge to allow any items with M1910 type wire hangers to be attached, either in place of the standard equipment belt or as additional stowage, although the extra weight was burdensome.

"blooperman" with an M79 grenade launcher—vital skills that increased squad survival. For several months, he was on top of his game, barring injury, tropical illness or the all too brief R&R, until he became a "short timer" when thoughts of returning to "The World" became uppermost in his mind. Now he was edgy and cautious in the field and once more a risk to himself and his comrades until the "Freedom Bird" flew him home stateside when the next FNG arrived. The whole process then started again. It was a truism of the war that the U.S. armed forces did not fight in Vietnam for eight years, but for one year eight times.

ABOVE: Marines of the H & S Company, 3/5 Marines, man a 106-mm recoilless rifle on 21 July 1969 during operations in the Que Son Mountains. Despite its weight of 400 pounds, the M40 provided a heavy punch in the field especially from hill-top positions such as this. With a .50-caliber spotting rifle above the weapon to mark the target, the 106-mm was accurate out to 1,200 yards.

LEFT: Commonly as young as 19 years old, the average Marine rifleman was cruelly burdened with equipment and ammunition when on operations in the field as evinced in the face of this exhausted Marine.

An M101A1 105-mm howitzer of Battery K, 3rd Battalion, 11th Marines, fires in support of Hotel Company, 3/5 Marines, during Operation Desoto on 21 February 1967. The M101 fired a 33-pound projectile to a maximum range of 12,500 yards. The waist-high breech of the weapon made it easy to load and allowed a sustained rate of fire of up to ten rounds a minute. The M101 could fire a wide variety of ammunition beside the standard high explosive (HE) round, including HEAT (high explosive anti-tank), smoke, white phosphorus, illuminating, chemical such as CS gas, propaganda leaflets, and the deadly anti-personnel flechette round to counter human-wave attacks or sapper infiltration of the perimeters of fire support bases. At 2½ tons it was a heavy weapon but at the same time rugged and reliable. Note the bunker in the background to shelter the gun crew during enemy indirect-fire attack.

dispatched on repeated pointless operations where they acted as ambush bait for a skilled, committed, and well-armed enemy well versed in small-unit tactics. It is therefore all the more remarkable that the "grunts" on the ground persisted for so long in the dutiful execution of a misguided military strategy and for an incompetent political leadership.

Whatever the circumstances, III MAF needed more troops to fulfil its stated mission and that required the full deployment of the 1st Marine Division to South Vietnam from Camp Courtney in Okinawa and Camp Pendleton in California. In January 1966, 1/11 and Battery K, 4/11, landed at Chu Lai with 2/11 arriving in May. The guns of 1/11, 3/11, and 4/11 provided artillery support throughout the expanding Chu Lai TAOR. On 28 March 1966, the divisional headquarters became operational at Chu Lai under the command of Maj. Gen. Lewis J. Fields. In the following weeks 1/5 and 2/5 arrived. At the same time, the division conducted some ten battalion-sized operations beyond the Chu Lai TAOR, but pacification programs remained a high priority as well. By the end of June, the TAOR had expanded from 205 square miles at the start of the year to 340.

Deep in the bush, men of Charlie Company, 1/7 Marines, check out their equipment following a firefight with the Viet Cong. Such thick vegetation gives a good indication of how difficult it was to control troops during a contact that might happen at almost point-blank range.

The 1st Marine Division now consisted of over 17,000 men with five infantry battalions from 5th and 7th Marines and four artillery battalions of 11th Marines, plus other supporting elements including amtrac, anti-tank, engineer, reconnaissance, and tank battalions. In May, divisional headquarters moved to Da Nang to take over the former 3rd Marine Division headquarters as the Marine Corps commitment moved northwards towards the DMZ. Meanwhile, the 3rd Marine Division retained control of two battalions of the 1st Marines, with the third acting as a floating reserve in the Special Landing Force. With the 11th Regiment now fully deployed, its main tasks were harassment and interdiction (H & I) missions with 1st Battalion generally in direct support of 1st Marines, 2/11 in support of 5th Marines, and 3/11 with 7th Marines, while 4th Battalion provided general artillery support.

During this frenetic period of deployment and operations for the division, there was a political insurrection in I CTZ with the "Buddhist Revolt" across the region. This highlighted the chronic fault line in South Vietnamese society between the Catholic political elite in Saigon and the vast majority of the population who were Buddhist. This followed the sacking of the Vietnamese commander of I Corps, Gen. Nguyen Chanh Thi, by Prime Minister Ky. ARVN units deployed against each other and against the people of the "Struggle Movement." A critical encounter between pro- and anti-government forces occurred just outside III MAF headquarters and disaster was only averted through protracted negotiations conducted by General Walt. Eventually the "Struggle Movement" was subdued by mid-June. This episode virtually paralyzed ARVN operations against the real enemy and also compromised months of Marine endeavors in the field as the Viet Cong re-established their cadres in many rural villages and hamlets. The Marines would have to recover the lost ground and try to re-establish government control. It was a task of Sisyphus.

(In Greek legend, Sisyphus was condemned for eternity to push a large boulder up a hillside but whenever he reached the top it rolled down again and he was obliged to repeat the process—much like a Marine encumbered with M1 steel helmet, bulky M1955 flak jacket, M60 machine gun, belts of ammunition, and a fully laden backpack trudging through the "boondocks" in the oppressive heat—day after day—searching for the VC during his 13-month tour of duty.)

I Corps Tactical Zone was the principal area of operations for the U.S. Marine Corps during the Vietnam War. The main airbases of 1 MAW are marked by appropriate aircraft symbols.

The Expanding War

Despite the political crisis in I CTZ during the first half of 1966, the war went on for the Marines as they undertook operations large and small. A classic example of the latter occurred in June during Operation Kansas when Team 2, 1st Platoon, Company C of the 1st Reconnaissance Battalion was operating deep inside enemy-dominated territory west of Chu Lai. Commanded by Staff Sgt. Jimmie E. Howard, a much-decorated Korean veteran, the 18-man unit was perched on top of the 1,500-foot Hill 488, or Nui Vu in Vietnamese, to observe enemy infiltration routes to the coast. From there they directed accurate artillery fire on to targets of opportunity until the enemy's suspicions were raised. During their third night in the observation post (OP) the Marines were attacked by a force of the 3rd NVA Regiment at midnight on 15 June. (The North Vietnamese Army or NVA was the common term used by the U.S. military for the People's Army of Vietnam or PAVN and NVA is used throughout the text. However, the Marines often referred to them as "pavins"— pronounced "par-vins"—although many other terms were used for the enemy in Marine Corps parlance.)

A four-man team in a forward listening post under Lance Cpl. Binns was struck first. Under a hail of automatic fire, Binns shot the closest enemy soldier while his team threw hand grenades before scrambling up to the crest to join the rest of the Marines. So close were the enemy that there was little time to reload. The Navy corpsman with the team, Billee Don Holmes, recalled "... they were within 20 feet of us. Suddenly there were grenades all over. Then people started hollering. It seemed everybody got hit at the same time." Holmes crawled forward to help an injured Marine when another grenade exploded and he was knocked unconscious. After emptying his rifle into the charging mass, Lance Cpl. John T. Adams used his M14 as a club, killing two more NVA before he was shot down. In bitter hand-to-hand fighting, Cpl. Jerrald R. Thompson was wounded by a grenade but he killed two with his combat knife before he was overwhelmed.

Four 12.7-mm heavy machine guns started to rake the position from the four points of the compass. The Marines were forced into an ever tighter perimeter among a stand of rocks and boulders as hand grenades and automatic fire continued to plunge down among the defenders while the NVA taunted them with cries of "Marines, you die! You die tonight!" like their fathers had heard from the Japanese in a previous war. These disturbing shouts were compounded by the strange and eerie sounds of clacking bamboo sticks as the NVA coordinated their assault against the unfortunate Marines. Howard was wounded in the legs and unable to move but he continued to direct the fight. Slumped beside the radio using his curious callsign of "Carnival Time," he brought in artillery fire, air strikes, and helicopter gunships against the encircling NVA under the piercing light of parachute flares dropped by a USAF C-47, callsign "Smoky Gold." The Hueys of VMO-6 strafed the enemy to within 20 yards of the perimeter while Marine fixed-wing aircraft dropped napalm within 100. With their ammunition expended, the Hueys then acted as TACAs or Tactical Air Controllers Airborne to direct the bombing runs of the "fast movers."

When ammunition ran low, the Marines on Nui Vu threw rocks and used captured weapons wrenched from the dead to return the enemy fire. When dawn broke six Marines were dead and all but one of the remainder wounded. With the first rays of light, helicopters of MAG-36 swooped in to evacuate the exhausted band of Marines but they were

"This is my rifle. There are many like it, but this one is mine. My rifle is my best friend. It is my life. I must master it as I must master my life. My rifle, without me, is useless. Without my rifle, I am useless ..." *The Creed of a U.S. Marine.* In this case the rifle is an M14 7.62-mm semi-automatic. At 11.1 pounds, the M14 was a heavy but powerful weapon with an equally powerful kick on firing. Beautifully engineered and highly accurate, the M14 was a fine weapon for the combat rifleman.

Green Marines:
African-Americans in the Corps

African-Americans made a major contribution to the Marine Corps in Vietnam as MOS 0311 Riflemen and in a host of other roles but racial discord remained a serious problem. Nevertheless, within a generation, an African-American and Vietnam Veteran, General Colin Powell, became Chairman of the Joint Chiefs of Staff, the supreme soldier in the US military.

THE VIETNAM WAR was the first racially integrated conflict fought by the U.S. armed forces. The U.S. Marine Corps was late to integrate African-Americans into its ranks. In the early 1960s, blacks represented 11 percent of the general population and by 1965 this was reflected demographically in the Marine Corps as 11.5 percent of the enlisted men were African-Americans. Prior to 1966, racial animosity within the Corps was not a readily apparent problem as all Marines were professional comrades in arms. However, there were only 48 black commissioned officers and just 184 in the top three enlisted ranks. The

U.S. armed forces were probably the most integrated of institutions in American society at the time but that did not mean that discrimination was not rife due to institutional racism. During the Vietnam War, Uncle Sam was certainly an equal opportunity employer but because of generations of underprivilege and neglected education, African-Americans figured disproportionately as infantrymen and in lowly support tasks in the supply services. During 1965–7, they constituted 23 percent of all Americans killed in action but were still proportionally 11 percent in the Marine Corps. Such figures fuelled accusations that the U.S. government was using blacks as cannon fodder at a time when Civil Rights had become such a leading issue in America. Black music was certainly not played 23 percent of the time on Armed Forces Radio Network, a typical example of the denial of African-American culture that many blacks felt deeply. The inequality of the Selective Service System meant that a larger proportion of impoverished blacks from urban ghettoes and poor whites from rural areas were drafted into the armed forces, while middle-class white males sought deferment through a college education or service with the National Guard; in 1968, only 1 percent of Army National Guardsmen were African-Americans.

In the USMC, it was axiomatic that a Marine was a Marine and the only colour that mattered was combat green; hence the title "Green Marines" was hailed as a denial of racial discrimination. In the field under fire such sentiments held true. There was no room for racism in a foxhole. Blacks, whites or Hispanics fought together and died together—"same

ABOVE: There was no room for racism in a foxhole. Out in the "boonies," black and white Marines shared all the miseries that Vietnam could throw at them and there were plenty of those.

mud, same blood." Five African-American Marines were awarded the Medal of Honor in Vietnam and all were killed shielding fellow Marines by throwing themselves on to exploding hand grenades. Yet, once back at base, racial tensions resurfaced and grew as the frustrating war progressed, reflecting the rise of Black Power and the increasing influence of the Black Muslim religion in America. The assassination of Dr Martin Luther King in April 1968 caused a major crisis in race relations, with riots both in America and in South Vietnam. The armed forces were no better equipped to solve long-standing inequities within society than any other institution, yet the Marine Corps certainly tried. In just ten months of 1969, the 1st Marine Division reported 79 racial assaults and three racially motivated fraggings. In one incident, a grenade was thrown into an enlisted men's club, killing one Marine and wounding 62 others. In December 1969, Marine Corps Commandant General Leonard Chapman announced: "There is no question we've got a problem." It was made apparent to top officers that overt racism within their command could damage their careers. Thereafter, formal grievance sessions were implemented and certain aspects of exclusive behavior were now tolerated such as "Afro" haircuts, "slave bracelets" made from jungle bootlaces, and the "dap"—an elaborate form of greeting among blacks. It was all part of the deeper malaise engendered by the Vietnam War and the volatile domestic politics at home, including the protracted process to withdraw from the conflict. Nevertheless, the Vietnam experience did not detract from the comradeship of the foxhole and the shared hazards of confronting a common foe, irrespective of race or creed. Despite the disproportionate hazards they faced, African-Americans re-enlisted in the military in far greater numbers than whites and remained highly motivated professionals. Indeed, one of the positive aspects of the Vietnam War was that African-American service personnel could no longer be considered as second-class Marines, soldiers, sailors, or airmen. They were now true American warriors with a career path that led to the very top.

BELOW: Reflecting the wide ethnic diversity of the Marine Corps, a First Nation Marine, Pfc. Joseph Big Medicine Jr. of the Cheyenne nation, writes a letter home during an operation conducted by Golf Company, 2/1 Marines, during July 1969. Note the K-Bar utility knife attached to his equipment belt and the olive-drab undershirt drapped over his shoulder. His ERDL pattern tropical trousers are rolled up to increase air circulation and keep cooler in the oppressive heat.

Marines of Company A, 1/7 Marines, advance in line abreast, towards a village fortified and occupied by the Viet Cong, on 22 September 1966 during Operation Golden Fleece in Quang Ngai Province. Note the cardboard box containing 100 7.62-mm rounds on the nearest man's left hip and the M17 Chemical-Biological Field Mask carrier below his left hand that rarely carried a gasmask in the field but usually extra ammunition clips or personal effects.

met with long streams of machine-gun fire. Howard waved them away and directed yet more fire support to create a safer landing zone, but enemy fire remained intense. Maj. William J. Goodsell, the commanding officer of VMO-6, brought his UH-1E to a hover over the hilltop but it was immediately hit as were Goodsell and his co-pilot. Although they managed to crash-land the aircraft, Goodsell died later of gunshot wounds. Another helicopter attempted a landing but its crew chief was killed.

Other helicopters flew in Company C, 1/5, to unload the troops at the base of the hill from where they advanced upwards, eliminating the NVA as they climbed. When they reached the top, Howard's men had just eight rounds left between them and every one alive was injured, some of them several times over. Yet still the battle raged on and four more Marines were killed or wounded. Eventually the fighting subsided around noon and the Marines were evacuated together with their dead as the Marine Corps does not leave the bodies of fallen comrades on the battlefield. In this heroic battle, Recon Team 2 suffered 100 percent casualties, a rare and unenviable record for any military unit, yet they kept fighting to the end. Rarer still every member of the 18-man team, dead or alive, received a medal for outstanding gallantry including 15 Silver Stars and two Navy Crosses for Lance Cpl. Binns and Navy Corpsman Holmes. The six dead were John Adams, Ignatius Carlisi, Thomas Glawe, James McKinney, Alcadio Mascarenas, and Jerrald Thompson—their names indicative of the ethnic diversity of the Marine Corps and by extension the country they served. For his exemplary leadership and fortitude in battle, Staff Sgt. Jimmie Howard was awarded the Medal of Honor. Hill 488 was renamed "Howard's Hill" on every Marine map thereafter.

Farther north in I CTZ, the 3rd Marine Division was fighting a fierce battle against the NVA 324B Division as it infiltrated into South Vietnam across the DMZ. This was the first time the NVA had violated the Demilitarized Zone in such strength in support of the Main Force VC units that had been badly mauled by the Marines during the spring. III MAF countered the incursion with Task Force Delta, comprising some 8,000 Marines and 3,000 ARVN soldiers. Operation Hastings began on 15 July in the vicinity of Cam Lo on Route 9, the major

After their widespread experience with flamethrowers in the Pacific War, the Marine Corps retained these weapons for much longer than other services. The standard crew-served flamethrower in Vietnam was the M2A1 that was issued in small numbers with approximately two per infantry battalion. Used by the "Zippo squad," the weapon had a range of almost 50 yards and was capable of firing up to ten one-second shots of flame. It was effective in clearing bunkers and tunnels as well as destroying enemy stores and huts but its considerable weight of 72 pounds made it impractical in the field. Indeed, the ready availability of air-delivered napalm rendered the man-portable flamethrower outmoded.

Close Air Support: 1st Marine Air Wing

Two F-4B Phantoms of VMFA-542 from MAG-11 of the 1st Marine Air Wing fly in formation on their way to attack targets in January 1969. VMFA-542 arrived at Da Nang on 10 July 1965 and commenced air operations shortly thereafter. Its primary mission was to provide air support to Marine ground forces. In August 1965, the squadron supported the 7th Marines in Operation Starlite, the first major American ground operation of the war. VMFA-542 conducted another three tours of duty in South Vietnam. It dropped over 20,000 tons of ordnance in SE Asia between May 1968 and January 1970. The last mission flown by the squadron was a night interdiction flight over Laos on 13 January 1970.

THE MARINE CORPS was quick to realize the military potential of aviation and acquired its first aircraft in 1912. However, following World War 1, military aviation was badly neglected due to lack of funds. In 1936, the Marine Corps had just 145 pilots but by the end of World War 2 the total had increased to over 10,000. Then and since, every pilot is a Marine first and foremost and all aviators have to undergo the same basic infantry training so that they never forget that their primary role is the support of the Marine combat rifleman on the ground. No other service devotes such priority to the concept of close air support from both fixed-wing and rotary-wing aircraft. Fundamental to this role is the ability of Marine fixed-wing aviation to provide close air support during an amphibious assault and during subsequent land operations. Accordingly, squadrons of Marine attack and fighter aircraft are deployed on U.S. Navy carriers for the task but inevitably these shipboard fixed-wing assets are limited in number and the provision of shore bases is a priority, as virtually every landing during the Pacific campaign of World War 2 demonstrated.

In Vietnam, the 1st Marine Air Wing was tasked with the direct support of the Marine divisions operating in I CTZ. It was not until the airbases at Da Nang and Chu Lai were fully operational in 1966 that this was truly possible. Thereafter, F-4 Phantoms and A-4 Skyhawks were on constant call to provide close air support

to Marines in contact on the ground as were UH-1 Huey gunships and medium helicopters for resupply and medical evacuation of casualties. Marine F-8 Crusaders provided top cover but in true Marine tradition also gave close air support with their 20-mm cannon, notably during the battles for Howard's Hill and Hue City. These aircraft came under the Marine Air Groups of 1 MAW. At the start of 1967, it comprised three fixed-wing groups, MAG-11, -12, and -13, and two rotary-wing groups, MAG-16 and -36. MAG-11 operated from Da Nang and MAG-12 and MAG-13 at Chu Lai. The helicopter squadrons were more dispersed with those of MAG-16 at Marble Mountain and Phu Bai, and MAG-36 at Ky Ha. In addition, there were numerous support squadrons, including transport and observation aircraft.

The compact and agile A-4 Skyhawk proved highly effective in the close air support role, delivering "snake and nape" within a few hundred yards of Marines in contact with the enemy—snake being Snakeye

fin-retarded bombs and nape being napalm canisters. While the Skyhawk or "Scooter" undertook the majority of CAS missions in the early years, the F-4 Phantom II provided heavier firepower with up to 16,000 pounds of bombs and rockets, more often than not directed on to the target by a forward air controller on the ground or airborne in a light aircraft such as the O-1 Bird Dog.

The A-4 and F-4 were the principal CAS aircraft during daylight hours but at night the A-6 Intruder came into its own. It was also highly effective during the bad weather that prevailed during the winter months, providing CAS to troops in contact and undertaking interdiction missions throughout Southeast Asia. The Marines also flew the EA-6 Prowler electronic warfare variant that became increasingly important as the air war progressed. It was generally recognized that Marine aviators provided the most effective and consistent close air support from fixed-wing aircraft for troops on the ground during the Vietnam War, reflecting the fact that the 1st Aircraft Wing was an integral part of III MAF and fundamental to all Marine operations on the ground.

With their tailhooks down, two Grumman A-6A Intruders of VA-85 prepare to land on the aircraft carrier USS *Kitty Hawk* in the South China Sea. The Intruder was flown by both the Navy and the Marine Corps and was capable of carrying some 15,000 pounds of ordnance. With its advanced avionics and all-weather capability, it was an outstanding attack aircraft during the Vietnam War and provided vital close air support to Marines on the ground even during the darkest of nights or the foulest of monsoon rains.

The coastal rice-growing plains were vital to the livelihoods of the South Vietnamese and became repeated battle grounds for the 1st Marine Division, particularly in the Que Son and An Hoa Valleys.

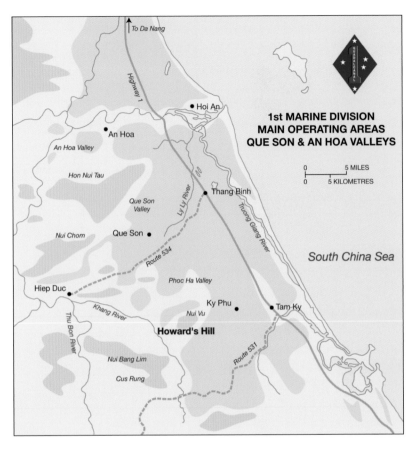

east–west road just below the DMZ, near a 700-foot hill called the Rock Pile that dominated the surrounding terrain and served as an important Marine OP. Prior to the operation, 2nd Battalion, 1st Marines, was employed extensively conducting reconnaissance to track enemy movements. In the days that followed 1/1 joined Task Force Delta as the operation went over to the offensive in the Song Ngan Valley.

At this time 3/5 Marines was part of the Special Landing Force seaborne reserve and it was landed by helicopter on 18 July in support of 2/4 and 3/4 Marines in various sweeps against persistent enemy resistance including an attack on Hill 208, which was suspected of being the command post of the 324B Division. Thereafter 2/1 and 3/5 Marines joined forces to establish blocking positions across enemy escape routes. Fighting flared and subsided over the coming days until 24 July when 3/5 encountered an NVA battalion on the jungle-covered Hill 362. While trying to establish a radio link on the hilltop, 2nd Platoon of Company I was confronted by enemy soldiers well entrenched in the jungle growth. In the first fusillade, the Marines suffered heavy casualties and the survivors went to ground. Because of the thick canopy, close air support was impossible and artillery bursts were rendered ineffective by the dense foliage. Lance Cpl. Richard A.

Pittman of the following 1st Platoon heard the cries of his trapped comrades. Putting down his rifle, he grabbed an M60 machine gun and several belts of ammunition and rushed forwards under the covering fire of other members of 1st Platoon. In quick succession two machine-gun posts opened up on him and he silenced them both with controlled bursts of his M60. Some 50 yards farther up the trail he came across the ground where most of the casualties had been incurred. Although taking fire from between 30 and 40 NVA soldiers, he returned fire from the middle of the trail, while those wounded who could crawled back to the safety of the 1st Platoon position. When Pittman's M60 jammed, he picked up an AK47 and continued to return fire. When his ammunition was exhausted he threw a final grenade and withdrew with the last of the walking wounded. Only the dead and severely injured remained but then the enemy began to strip the dead bodies and, according to Lance Cpl. Raymond L. Powell, one of the few of the injured to survive, systematically shot ". . . anyone that moved. It was darn near like a massacre. I pretended I was dead when they got to me. They took my cigarettes and my watch, but they didn't shoot me."

The battle raged on with enemy efforts now directed against the rest of Company I digging in on the hilltop. They remained under constant mortar fire for the next two hours until a Marine UH-1E gunship of

The Marine Corps procured 700 M40 sniper rifles and approximately 200 were sent to Vietnam but, as of December 1969, only 23 remained serviceable. Here, a scout scans for a suitable target as the sniper uses his M1 helmet as a rest for his M40 rifle, a standard technique as wearing a helmet interfered with accurate shooting when lying in the prone position. Elaborate camouflage suits, much favored by snipers today, were rarely used in Vietnam. Although basically a standard civilian hunting rifle, the M40 proved highly effective in its sniping role. The two top-scoring snipers of the 1st Marine Division during the Vietnam War, Sgt. Chuck Mawhinney and Sgt. Carlos Hathcock, achieved 196 confirmed kills between them.

Marines shield their ears as they fire an M29 81-mm mortar at a fire support base. The "Eighty-One" was the standard infantry mortar of the Vietnam War. Weighing a total of 122 pounds, it was intended to be man-portable in the field when broken down into four parts but in the appalling terrain and climate conditions of Vietnam this became increasingly infrequent as fire support bases proliferated. The weapon was able to fire a wide variety of shells including HE, illuminating, smoke, and white phosphorus, all with adjustable fuses; for instance, a delayed-action fuse was necessary to penetrate thick jungle growth before exploding or else the round's explosive effect was wasted in the treetops. An experienced crew could drop 25 shells a minute on target out to a maximum range of three miles.

VMO-2 temporarily suppressed the enemy weapons. Company K was sent to assist but was ambushed in turn and its advance faltered. Beside enemy mortar bombs and automatic fire, the Marines were now bombarded by torrential rain as Typhoon Ora struck the region, further hampering operations. In these atrocious conditions, Marine combat engineers were lowered from helicopters to blast improvised landing zones with explosives to allow the evacuation of the wounded, but MAG-16 helicopters were only able to extract 16 wounded of Company K before nightfall.

Company I was now forced to spend "one long night on Hill 362" under repeated attack from the NVA who often closed within 15–20 feet of the company perimeter. Marine Cpl. Mark E. Whieley recalled: "The Commies were so damn close we could hear them breathing heavily and hear them talking." But by dawn the NVA had broken contact and the two Marine companies were able to link up on top of Hill 362. Company I had suffered exactly 100 casualties, with 18 dead and 82 wounded out of an assigned strength of 130. For his consummate bravery during the battle for Hill 362, Lance Cpl. Pittman was awarded the Medal of Honor. On 30 July, 3/5 returned to sea as the SLF.

Operation Hastings continued until 3 August when it was terminated. It was the largest and most hard-fought operation of the war so far in I CTZ. The Marines lost 126 killed and 448 wounded while the ARVN suffered 12 killed and 40 wounded. Enemy casualties were heavy, but as always difficult to verify. General Walt summed up this first major engagement with the NVA as follows: "We found them well equipped, well trained, and aggressive to the point of fanaticism. They attacked in mass formations and died by the hundreds. Their leaders had misjudged the fighting ability of U.S. Marines and ARVN soldiers together; our superiority in artillery and total command of the air."

Nevertheless, the Marines were being drawn inexorably towards the hinterland below the DMZ and away from the coastal enclaves where their pacification efforts had been effective and beneficial to many South Vietnamese civilians. Heavy fighting between the 3rd Marine Division and the NVA continued sporadically through the summer along the DMZ during Operation Prairie, which opened the day after Hastings closed and lasted for the remainder of the year. This essentially set the scene for the rest of the conflict with 3rd Marine Division fighting a mostly conventional war in Quang Tri Province with much of the fighting in an area bounded by Dong Ha, Cam Lo, Con Thien, and Gio Linh—the fabled "Leatherneck Square." The intense fighting in the final months caused deep concern to General Westmoreland and MACV in Saigon. He was particularly alarmed by the possibility of NVA forces outflanking the Marine defensive positions across the DMZ through the forbidding mountainous terrain of northwest Quang Tri

The film actress Ann-Margret performs in a USO show for III MAF at Chu Lai in March 1966. Such shows were popular with the troops and places were given as prizes in some units for good performance in the field such as finding an enemy weapons cache or a confirmed body count. The famous Bob Hope Show was guaranteed a full house with troops being flown in from a cross-section of the military formations in-country. In 1966 alone his show was seen by almost half the American troops in Southeast Asia.

The architects of failure—Robert S. McNamara (*center*) was the Secretary for Defense under President John F. Kennedy and he retained his appointment under President Lyndon B. Johnson. Seconded from the Ford Motor Company, McNamara was a true believer in high-technology weapons and systems analysis that gave rise to the concept of the "body count." A firm advocate of the "graduated response," he micro-managed the air campaign against North Vietnam to the point of impotency. He routinely ignored the advice of the Joint Chiefs of Staff who, to their shame, did little to challenge his misguided management of the war. He subsequently became disillusioned with the war and admitted that he "misunderstood the nature of the conflict." That misunderstanding cost the lives of over 50,000 Americans and innumerable people in Southeast Asia.

Province bordering Laos. To forestall such a move, Westmoreland suggested that III MAF should deploy a battalion in the heart of this rugged terrain at a place called Khe Sanh.

Ever mindful that his troops were being drawn even farther from the vital population centers, General Walt resisted the pressure from MACV. As General English, the 3rd Marine Division Assistant Divisional Commmander, declaimed: "When you're at Khe Sanh, you're not really anywhere. It's far from everything. You could lose it and you really haven't lost a damn thing." The simmering tensions between MACV and III MAF now came to the fore. Against his better instincts, General Walt ordered 1/3 Marines to establish a base at Khe Sanh and coordinate their operations with the U.S. Army Special Forces and ARVN troops in the area. MACV remained convinced that the NVA was preparing for a major incursion across the DMZ into "Marineland" as Saigon called I CTZ. As the 3rd Marine Division moved northwards so the 1st Marine Division followed to take over the vacated TAORs, with U.S. Army units now taking over areas of southern I CTZ for the first time. The emphasis of Marine operations was being made to conform with General Westmoreland's plan for 1967 to be the year of the big battles against the VC/NVA, who would be annihilated by massive firepower in the border areas that were largely free of civilians—that is discounting the aboriginal hill tribes, but then all sides did that anyway except the Special Forces.

On 14 October 1966, just 18 months after the Marines first landed at Da Nang, Secretary of Defense Robert S. McNamara briefed President Johnson after a personal visit to South Vietnam: "There is no sign of an impending break in enemy morale and it appears that he can more than replace his losses . . . Pacification is a bad disappointment . . . full security exists nowhere—not even behind the U.S. Marines' lines and in Saigon; in the countryside, the enemy almost completely controls the night." Yet General Westmoreland's whole military strategy was predicated on inflicting such a rate of casualties on the enemy through firepower and attrition that they must inevitably be defeated on the battlefield. And the battlegrounds that Westmoreland chose were the border regions with Cambodia, Laos, and North Vietnam itself, and the Central Highlands, "a run of erratic mountain ranges, gnarled

With his M1911A1 automatic pistol readily to hand, a Marine fills his water canteen as he crosses a river. Attached to his rucksack is another M1910 canteen. Water was a vital commodity in the sweltering heat of Vietnam and canteens were replenished at every opportunity, even from the brackish water of a river in the field. Across his shoulders is an ammunition tube for an M28A2 HEAT 3.5-inch rocket launcher round or 81-mm mortar shell. Although bulky and heavy, the M20 rocket launcher was widely used by Marines in the field in the early years of the war to destroy enemy bunkers.

valleys, jungled ravines, and abrupt plains" that ran like a spine up the western edge of South Vietnam. These were some of the most inhospitable areas imaginable for a Western soldier where even the vaunted tactical advantages of overwhelming firepower and helicopter air mobility were compromised by heat, altitude, and terrain. Worse still, it conformed exactly to the strategy of Westmoreland's formidable opponent General Vo Nguyen Giap who indicated: "The primary emphasis is to draw American units into remote areas and thereby facilitate control of the population of the lowlands."

Grunts and Gunners:
11th Marine Regiment

FIRE AND MANEUVER remain the basic tenets of warfare. It is the function of firepower to allow troops to maneuver on the battlefield and gain positional advantage. Artillery provides the most efficient application of firepower both to destroy an enemy in place and deny him the ability to maneuver freely. During the Vietnam War, field artillery was employed on a prodigious scale in support of troops on the ground. Any infantry squad with a radio to hand could call on artillery support within a matter of minutes across the length and breadth of South Vietnam, a remarkable battlefield achievement by any standards. In the Marine Corps, each division had an integral artillery regiment that provided consistent and dedicated fire support to the three infantry regiments. Again the ethos of the Corps demanded that support to the combat rifleman on the ground was paramount so it was common practice for individual artillery battalions to fight with specific infantry regiments for extended periods of time in order to increase familiarity and flexibility.

Located at Camp Muir on Hill 55, an M107 175-mm Self-Propelled Gun of the 1st 175-mm Gun Battery (SP) of 4/11 Marines during a fire mission in support of the 7th Marines. The M107 fired a 174-pound projectile to a distance of 20 miles, making it the longest-range artillery weapon in U.S. service in South Vietnam.

Marine artillery battalions were often dispersed in far-flung firebases or deployed in all manner of terrain so their organization tended to change according to the tactical situation. The basic tool of the battalion was the towed M101A1 105-mm light howitzer based on a design from World War 2. These were supplemented by the M1A1, and later M114, 155-mm medium howitzer and similar weapons on self-propelled mountings—the M53 and subsequently the M109. Heavier weapons of 175-mm and 8-inch caliber were attached to the regiment depending on the particular fire mission or operation, with some of these pieces being provided by the U.S. Army in the form of the M107 and M110 self-propelled guns. These heavier weapons were usually grouped in the 4th or general support battalion of the artillery regiment. Fundamental to the provision of instant fire support was the establishment of self-contained artillery firebases across a formation's TAOR. The smallest of these might contain a single battery of six 105-mm howitzers, with a number of 120-mm or 81-mm mortars for close-in defense and area support. These weapons were controlled by a fire direction center, which liaised directly with the troops on the ground. Firebases were normally positioned in range of each other so that mutually supporting fires were available in case of attack and to provide greater firepower to the maneuver battalions in the field. By 1970, the 11th Marines had 65 fire support bases in Quang Nam Province alone.

As the war progressed, firepower came to dominate over maneuver on the basis that "bullets, not bodies" should be expended on the battlefield; this accorded with the overriding strategy of attrition. In January 1970, the 11th fired 178,062 rounds during 19,250 fire missions from the 156 tubes at its disposal. In the same month, six naval ships fired 5,541 rounds in support of ground operations, highlighting another important aspect of Marine fire support. Originally intended to support amphibious landings, naval gunfire was a useful adjunct to Marine firepower—from the 5-inch guns of destroyers up to the 16-inch guns of the battleship USS *New Jersey* whose shells each weighed one ton. To utilize all available firepower to the full, the Marines employed Air–Naval Gunfire Liaison Companies or ANGLICOs, which were teams specially trained in fire support coordination using specialized long-range communications equipment. Whatever the means, the primary purpose remained the support of the combat rifleman with the heaviest firepower in the shortest possible time.

ABOVE: Gunners of the 11th Marines, "The Cannon Cockers," in action at a fire support base. Because there were no fixed frontlines, fire support bases were a significant tactical innovation in the Vietnam War and their guns had to provide all-round fire support. Some of the costliest engagements of the war for American forces were when firebases came under determined attack. For these circumstances the M101 howitzer was provided with "beehive" rounds that were like giant shotgun shells carrying thousands of steel flechettes that shredded troops exposed in the open.

LEFT: An M53 155-mm Self-Propelled Gun of the 1st 155 Gun Platoon near Phu Bai on 7 February 1967. The M53 was based on components of the M47/M48 series medium tanks, with the engine and transmission at the front of the vehicle and the large gun turret at the rear. The entire crew was housed in the turret with the driver stationed at the front left of the turret. The M55 8-inch self-propelled howitzer used the same chassis and the M86 gun mount could accept either weapon, with ammunition stowage racks being interchangeable between the two vehicles. The U.S. Army converted all of its M53s to M55s from 1956, but the Marine Corps continued to use the M53 configuration in the early years of the Vietnam War.

(As with many military memoirs, those of General Giap are partial and self-serving but he was a remarkable commander irrespective of his political persuasion and his observations deserve close scrutiny.)

Pacification

In 1966, the CIA estimated that there were just 38,000 NVA soldiers in South Vietnam together with at most 250,000 Viet Cong or NLF (National Liberation Front) insurgents. The latter were conducting a classic campaign of guerrilla warfare using hit-and-run tactics against targets of opportunity and slipping away whenever the opposition was too strong or their firepower too damaging. Despite the protestations of the Saigon government, the insurgents received much succor from the rural and urban populace through either commitment, coercion, or calculation. In the words of General Giap: "Without the people we have no information … They hide us, protect us, feed us and tend our wounded." Accordingly the VC did not require much outside support beyond essential arms and ammunition; a further CIA study of 1965 estimated that the VC needed no more than 12 tons of supplies a day from outside South Vietnam. This equated to the load of a single tractor-trailer rig or less than the daily provision by truck of a typical American suburban supermarket.

Accompanied by A-7C Corsairs of VA-86, F-4B Phantom II fighter bombers of VF-161 flying from the USS *Midway* unleash their Mk 82 bombs through moderate cloud cover by Loran attack during a mission "up north" as part of Operation Linebacker I in May 1972. The successful air campaigns of Operations Linebacker I and II during May and December 1972 were directed at the North Vietnamese transportation system and the strategic targets in and around Hanoi and Haiphong, the very targets advocated by Marine Corps commanders as early as 1965.

A cornerstone of the conduct of the air war was the massive interdiction of the Ho Chi Minh Trail as it wended its way from North Vietnam through Laos and Cambodia to the borders of South Vietnam; this was the presumed primary source of communist supplies into the south. Yet a significant proportion of these supplies reached South Vietnam by sea since the vast majority of the population lived in coastal regions where the insurgents were most active. It was so much easier to hide a few hundredweight of 7.62-mm ammunition or a few dozen rocket-propelled grenades (RPGs) in a sampan or fishing boat than have to use scores of porters to carry the same load over hundreds of miles of hostile terrain.

Lt. Gen. Victor "Brute" Krulak, commander of Fleet Marine Force, Pacific, and Maj. Gen. Lewis W. Walt, commander of III MAF, realized this implicitly from the outset. With the Marine Corps' long experience of small "colonial" wars, they immediately orchestrated initiatives of "pacification" across the coastal enclaves with the object of separating the people from the insurgents. As South Vietnam was primarily an agrarian society with the bulk of the population living in hamlets and villages, this meant committing troops down to the very basic level for an extended period of time so that the peasants who were tied to the land would come to trust the military and by extension the remote

Troops of 1/1 Marines search a manure pile for weapons during an operation near Marble Mountain in November 1966. Working in conjunction with ARVN units, County Fair was a continuing pacification mission to cordon and search villages to root out weapons and insurgents without causing too much distress to the inhabitants. While Marines usually managed the cordon, Vietnamese troops conducted the searches and government officials verified the identity of villagers, with medical care being provided by a Navy corpsman. The Marine in the foreground is an RTO—radio telephone operator—with an AN/PRC-25 FM radio on his back, a type that had only just been introduced into the Marine Corps. Note the bag attached to the radio that contained the sections of the long-range antenna, handset and spare parts for the radio. As an RTO he carries an M1911A1 automatic pistol as a personal weapon.

Members of the 306th Regional Forces and a Combined Unit Pacification Platoon of 2/5 Marines undertake a cordon and search operation south of Da Nang on 29 December 1970. Pacification was an important role for the Marine Corps throughout its presence in South Vietnam.

government in Saigon. Only once the people were confident in their own security and livelihoods would they provide the essential intelligence to allow government and allied forces to root out the insurgents—by force if necessary or better still by persuasion that the traditional South Vietnamese way of life under a "democratic" government was preferable to that of a hostile communist regime imposed from the North.

In conjunction with the U.S. Navy, the Marine Corps was well suited to perform both the tasks of pacification and interdicting infiltration by sea. On 31 July 1965, the U.S. Navy Task Force 115 or the Coastal Surveillance Force assumed full responsibility for Operation Market Time to counter enemy seaborne supply movements along the

1,200 miles of South Vietnamese coastline. The Navy devised a three-tier scheme with aerial patrols together with Coastguard and Navy vessels as an outer barrier and an inner barrier of smaller fast patrol craft such as Swift Boats to stop and search the innumerable junks, sampans, and fishing boats sailing along the coastline. When combined with Marine Special Landing Forces to pursue infiltrators ashore, the Navy was able to keep a tight rein on seaborne infiltration in I CTZ.

On the day after the formation of the Coastal Surveillance Force, the Joint Action Company, subsequently the Combined Action Company or CACO, was officially formed at Phu Bai to coordinate Marine pacification efforts. It comprised five South Vietnamese "Ruff-Puff" (Regional Forces and Popular Forces—RF/PF) platoons each reinforced by a Marine infantry squad, subsequently termed Combined Action Platoons (CAP). These units were deployed in the many villages in I CTZ to provide security for their inhabitants on a long-term basis. At its height the Combined Action Program fielded four battalions of CAPs. It was common practice for the Ruff-Puffs to be stationed in their home areas where their local knowledge was significant and their motivation to defend them greater. A full-strength platoon comprised one officer and 37 PF troops organized into three 11-men squads and a five-man HQ squad. The CAP combined a PF platoon with a 14-man Marine rifle squad, usually commanded by a sergeant, and a Navy corpsman to provide medical aid to the villagers. The Marine NCO acted as an advisor to the Vietnamese platoon leader while one each of the three Marine fire teams was assigned to a PF squad.

By these means the Marines became deeply involved with local activities and grew to know the surrounding terrain intimately,

Riflemen of Company G, 2/1 Marines, scan the treeline for the enemy after suspicious noises were heard during a break in a clear and search operation on 21 July 1969, hence the lack of body armor and fighting equipment. Troops took every opportunity to divest themselves of their equipment, which commonly weighed up to 60 pounds in the field. Trying to climb to one's feet with such a load to resume a mission inevitably resulted in an involuntary "grunt," hence the term that came to describe all American soldiers and Marines in Vietnam.

A Marine probes a waterhole during a cordon and search operation conducted by Delta Company, 1/1 Marines, and Mike Company, 3/1 Marines, near Marble Mountain, the home of the Marine helicopter squadrons of MAG-36, on 8 November 1966. The Viet Cong were highly adept at hiding contraband of all sorts, particularly weapons. Wrapped in plastic and hidden underwater for prolonged periods of time, an AK47 assault rifle remained ready for use at a moment's notice for the committed VC soldier.

minimizing the risk of booby-traps and maximizing the opportunities to ambush insurgents. Initially there were significant problems as Ruff-Puff troops were at the bottom of the ARVN supply chain and would be lucky to have M1 Carbines rather than old Japanese or French bolt-action rifles. Their pay was pitiful (less than $10 a month) and inconsistent. Uniforms were virtually non-existent. Accordingly they tended to wear the traditional peasant garb of black pyjamas, which did lead to confusion of identity with the VC. It was common practice for CAP leaders to brief Marine patrol commanders and pilots to the effect that: "If you can see them in black pyjamas, they are Ruff-Puffs and if you can't, they're Viet Cong."

In time, and time is the essence in successful counterinsurgency warfare, the CAPs became highly effective despite MACV's concerns that they were extremely vulnerable to enemy attack, particularly at night when ready reaction forces would be more difficult to deploy in support. As a case in point, the coastal village of Binh Nghia in the Chu Lai TAOR serves as good example. (The classic account of this action appears in *The Village* by Marine Captain Francis J. West Jr. published by Harper & Row of New York in 1972.) Binh Nghia in the Binh Son district was a collection of seven hamlets with some 5,000 inhabitants of whom some 750 had joined the VC, so it was hardly a pro-government village. A Marine CAP led by Cpl. Robert A. Beebe from Company C, 1st Battalion, 7th Marines, first arrived there on 12 June 1966 where it joined up with 15 local policemen and 18 PF troops. They set up camp in an old house that had been abandoned by a rich landowner in 1950 when the Viet Minh (forerunner of the Viet Cong) took over the area. After fortifying the villa during the day, the Marines conducted a night patrol. The VC were obliged to respond to the Marines' presence or else see their influence crumble among the people. A VC assassination squad entered Binh Nghia and killed the village chief. At the end of the month, the Marines suffered their first casualty when Pfc. Lawrence L. Page was killed in an ambush while on a night patrol, yet the Marines remained and renamed the fortified villa "Fort Page" in his honor.

After many days and nights of intensive patrolling, the Marines gained their revenge in a well-executed ambush. In a brief firefight lasting just eight minutes, a patrol of five Marines and three PF troops killed 21 VC while suffering no casualties themselves. Over the next two months, the CAP averaged 11 firefights a month and then these tailed off as the Marines gained dominance on the ground but the VC were not about to admit it. On the night of 14 September, a company of approximately 60 men of the 409th NVA Battalion together with 80 local Viet Cong attacked Fort Page while several Marines and PF troops were on patrol. In a bitterly contested battle, five Marines and the Navy corpsman were killed while the only other Marine was wounded as were five of the 12 PF troops. The latter kept fighting until a reaction force from Company C, 1/7, arrived together with the rest of the CAP and the VC broke contact. On the following day, the remaining Marines of the CAP were given the option to leave Binh Nghia but, despite their losses, they elected to stay. As one Marine stated: "We couldn't leave. What would we have said to the PFs after the way we pushed them to fight the Viet Cong? We had to stay. There wasn't one of us who wanted to leave."

That day the villagers held a funeral service to honor the Marines and PF troops who had died in the defense of Fort Page. Six replacement Marines, all volunteers, joined the Binh Nhgia CAP immediately. It was a timely arrival. On the night of 16 September the Viet Cong returned, expecting no resistance. They strolled down the main path through the village towards the market place only to bump into a CAP patrol. In the ensuing firefight ten VC were confirmed dead with an unknown number killed as they tried to flee across the Song Tra Bong bordering the south of the village. There were no Marine or PF casualties in this action. The Marines were by now becoming closely

Widely dispersed to prevent multiple casualties in case of a booby-trap explosion, Marines of Company I, 3rd Battalion, 1st Marines, cross waterlogged paddy fields on 19 November 1966. Unusually these Marines are not wearing body armor during an operation in the field.

integrated into the life of the village and "... the five thousand villagers accepted them. They ate in their houses, went to their parties and to their funerals." Life for the villagers was much enhanced as no air strikes or artillery barrages were called in on Binh Nhgia because of the Marine presence there.

Sweltering in the heat and humidity, troops of Company G, 2/7 Marines, trudge across a paddy field in Quang Ngai Province on 29 July 1966. Most have an issue olive-drab towel around their necks to act as a sweat rag and as a cushioning material under equipment straps or weapons.

But the resolute Viet Cong were not ready to give up yet. In March 1967 another main-force attack of 300 VC was planned against Fort Page but local villagers informed the CAP. The Marines were ordered to evacuate Binh Nhgia in the face of such a threat but they refused, even if by disobeying orders they risked court martial. As one Marine pledged: "I'm going to stay here and blast them. They're not getting this fort. They're not getting this ville." And it did not happen. When one of the VC scouts was shot dead by an alert PF sentry, the attack was called off and the communists never again seriously threatened Binh Nhgia. After the Marines left in October 1967, village life continued in the time-honored fashion that the inhabitants desired with security provided by the Ruff-Puffs as was their principal purpose "... the PFs were patrolling ... in teams of two, like cops on a beat." There were clashes with the communists but the PF troops were largely able to keep them at bay.

Binh Nhgia was by no means unique. General Krulak later wrote: "No village protected by a Combined Action Platoon was ever repossessed by the Viet Cong and 60 per cent of the Marines serving in Combined Action units volunteered to stay on with their Marine and Vietnamese companions for an additional six months when they could have returned to the United States." By the end of 1966, there were 58 Combined Action Platoons in being, but that was not nearly enough to meet the requirement. As U.S. Ambassador Henry Cabot said at the time on the scale of the problems in South Vietnam: "In this war, when we have beaten the Army of North Vietnam and the Main Force battalions of the Viet Cong, we have simply won the opportunity to get at the heart of the matter, which is more than 150,000 terrorist guerrillas highly organized throughout the country and looking like civilians." The only practical way to do this was through pacification programs on the ground using troops who were familiar with the inhabitants and topography of the villages in their charge, as well as with their culture and language, like the Marines of 1/7 in Binh Nhgia and their Ruff-Puff comrades in arms. However, because of the prevailing MACV policy, the Marine Corps was never able to devote the necessary resources to pacification. At its peak the program involved approximately 2,500 Marines. In 1970, the USMC pacification program was undertaken by Combined Action Groups employing a Marine company and a Ruff-Puff battalion. The last such unit was

With his M14 rifle readily to hand across his lap, a Marine takes a breather among the elephant grass out in the "boondocks," an old Marine term for any rough terrain that derives from the Tagalog word for "mountain" adopted as Marine slang after the 19th-century Philippines campaign. It also gave rise to the name of the popular "boonie" hat worn by this Marine in preference to the heavy M1 helmet. He is leaning on his lightweight tropical rucksack carried over his OG107 utility uniform.

A Marine prepares 107-mm mortar rounds for an M98 Howtar prior to a fire mission during Operation Deckhouse VI in February 1967. The Howtar was an artillery weapon peculiar to the Marine Corps. It combined the carriage of the 1930s vintage 75-mm M1 pack howitzer and the M30 4.2-inch (107-mm) mortar. Accordingly, the Howtar weighed approximately one-fifth as much as a contemporary M101 howitzer but the explosive charge of the 107-mm mortar bomb was almost equivalent to the 105-mm HE round. The weapon could be carried inside a CH-46 Sea Knight, towed by a light truck, or even manhandled ashore during amphibious landings. In extreme situations, it could be broken down into man-portable sections. The Marine Corps adopted this interesting weapon in 1962 and each direct-support artillery battalion included one six-gun battery of Howtars.

withdrawn in the spring of 1971 by when all the successes had withered on the vine of MACV indifference.

One Army officer, Lt. Col. Jean Sauvageot, who worked on pacification programs in South Vietnam for several years, noted: "There was absolutely no comparison between CAP and what most Army units were doing. For example if CAP killed 15 enemy soldiers, they usually had 15 weapons to show for it. At the same time, Army units were killing 15 or 5 or 50 enemies and might not have a single weapon to show when the firing stopped . . . they were killing non-combatants and claiming them as dead enemy soldiers." In the U.S. Army, pacification was given a low priority, as it did not fit into General Westmoreland's overall campaign strategy. In his memoirs General Westmoreland claimed: "I simply had not enough numbers to put a squad of Americans in every village and hamlet."

Again, CIA statistics are revealing as in 1966 they estimated that there were 11,000 hamlets and villages in South Vietnam of which just over 5,000 were under government control, some 2,500 were contested, and almost 3,500 were in VC hands. By simple math, to place a 15-man squad in every village would have required 165,000 men—far fewer than the 540,000 American troops at the height of deployment in South Vietnam. To place more men in contested areas and villages would still not have required an inordinately greater number of troops.

Moreover, MACV's contention that CAPs were highly vulnerable and liable to suffer unacceptable casualties proved erroneous. USMC casualty returns reveal a 50 percent lower rate for Marines on CAP duties than those on search and destroy missions. But General Westmoreland wanted more of the latter and III MAF had no choice but to comply.

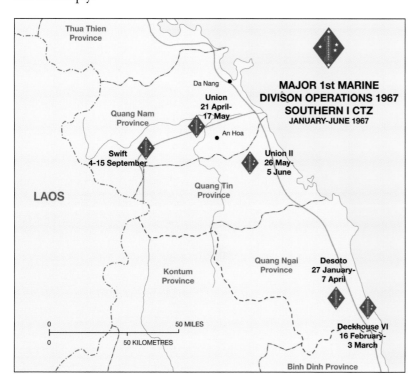

For General Westmoreland and MACV 1967 was the year of the big battles and 111 MAF despite serious reservations had to comply with the overall strategy.

1967 The Year of the Big Battles

By the start of 1967, the Marine Corps was essentially fighting two different wars in I CTZ. In the north the 3rd Marine Division was conducting almost conventional operations against NVA regular units along the DMZ while to their south the 1st Marine Division was embarked on a counterinsurgency campaign against VC guerrillas, although the 2nd NVA Division remained a constant adversary. This would continue into 1967 but with the emphasis now on General Westmoreland's "Big Battle" concept of search and destroy operations using U.S. units almost exclusively. This was codified in the 1967 Joint Combined Campaign Plan as endorsed at the Manila Conference where President Johnson declared: "I believe there is light at the end of what has been a long and lonely tunnel."

Throughout the Eisenhower and Kennedy years, millions of dollars were expended to create the ARVN as a clone of the U.S. Army to contain a concerted invasion from North Vietnam in a repeat of the Korean War. Accordingly it lacked the techniques, training, skills, or

Recon: The Elite of the Elite

A recon team member stands ready to conduct another reconnaissance mission. His headgear or "cover" is an unofficial locally produced camouflage "boonie hat." Camouflage face paint was commonly worn on patrol to blend into jungle terrain. He is armed with an M14 7.62-mm rifle and attached to his webbing harness a late model "K-Bar" fighting knife; note the discreet corporal's chevrons on the scabbard denoting his rank. As with many Marines, he has acquired the U.S. Army M1956/M1967 Load Carrying Equipment that was deemed superior to the Marine version. His equipment belt is festooned with hand grenades and extra water bottles and his pockets stuffed with items for maximum self-sufficiency in the field.

WHILE THE U.S. MARINE CORPS considers itself the elite of the U.S. armed forces, so the reconnaissance units of the Corps consider themselves to be the elite of the elite. This was particularly so in the Vietnam War. One of the most frustrating aspects of the conflict was the lack of accurate and timely intelligence concerning enemy units. Their ability to blend into the local population or disperse into hidden base areas was arguably the greatest impediment to mounting successful operations against the NVA or VC. The Marine Corps employed two types of reconnaissance units in Vietnam. Each division had an integral reconnaissance battalion tasked with gaining tactical intelligence within the divisional TAOR. For deeper strategic reconnaissance, III MAF employed force reconnaissance companies. Traditionally these had conducted beach reconnaissance before an amphibious landing and long-range patrolling in the subsequent land campaign, often behind enemy lines.

In Vietnam, the 1st and 3rd Reconnaissance Companies were directed by the III MAF Surveillance and Reconnaissance Center in their deep penetration patrols to enemy base areas and elsewhere during which they directed the full gamut of U.S. firepower on the enemy from tube artillery up to B-52 Arclight raids. The 1st Reconnaissance Battalion comprised four companies, each of approximately 150 men. On occasion it was reinforced to increase flexibility as in early 1970 when A Company, 5th Reconnaissance Battalion, was attached. Typically, a reconnaissance patrol comprised a team of six Marines. They would be inserted by helicopter, usually into the mountainous areas on the western edge of the divisional TAOR where NVA infiltration routes were most numerous. Each team included an officer or NCO patrol leader, a radioman, three specially trained riflemen and a Navy corpsman. Each team member carried roughly 70 pounds of equipment, ammunition, and food for up to six days. On their return to base, the team spent a day cleaning their weapons and equipment, a second day on training, and a third in preparing for another patrol which began on the next day. For most of 1970, the 1st Reconnaissance Battalion fielded 48 such teams with approximately half on patrol at any one time. During June 1970, it conducted 130 patrols and sighted 834 enemy, while directing 120 artillery fire missions and 25 air strikes, resulting in 198 enemy killed at a cost of 2 Marine dead and 15 wounded as well as 9 non-battle casualties.

As with most special forces units, recon teams tried to avoid contact with the enemy during their surveillance patrols. However, one standard technique was to set ambushes for small enemy units in order to capture prisoners for intelligence purposes. Nevertheless, the principal missions were intelligence-gathering and Stingray operations. The latter involved searching for enemy base camps or infiltration routes and putting them under covert observation until a suitable moment came to call in artillery and air strikes. Deep inside enemy-dominated territory, recon was a dangerous and harrowing assignment and only the elite were up to the task.

organization to counter the guerrilla tactics of the VC. It was now required to abandon its conventional guise and assume responsibility for conducting a counterinsurgency campaign just as the VC/NVA were gearing up for larger-scale operations. The bulk of the ARVN was to be deployed at the local level to implement pacification programs away from the safety of their fortified outposts, firebases, and comfortable quarters in the larger towns and cities where nefarious commercial opportunities were far greater. It was a role for which the ARVN was culturally and temperamentally unsuited. Unlike in the Korean War, there was no unified command in South Vietnam with all allied troops under a single commander, thus General Westmoreland never had the same freedom of maneuver or direction as General Douglas MacArthur. In addition, he suffered far greater political interference from both Washington and Saigon. It made a near-impossible war all the more difficult to conduct.

At the start of 1967, III MAF comprised 70,378 troops with 67,729 Marines and 2,649 sailors. Lt. Gen. Walt and his high command remained unhappy with the direction of the war by MACV. As he stated: "This is a political war, second a psychological war, and third a military war." But, in the unhappy phrase of the time, "It's the only war we got," and no military man, Marine or Army, was going to pass up the opportunity for any type of field command that would help to "get his

Although the hinterland of Vietnam is often stunningly beautiful, its many waterways, rugged mountains, and impenetrable jungle terrain were a serious impediment to troop movement on the ground, a fact often forgotten by commanders flying at 3,000 feet in their cool, breezy helicopters. Progress across difficult terrain was often in the order of just a thousand yards a day.

Sheltering behind a paddy field dike, Marines of Kilo Company, 3/5 Marines, provide a base of fire as other members of the unit assault enemy positions on the opening day of Operation Desoto, 27 January 1967.

ticket punched" for promotion. With the monsoon at its height, it was a relatively quiet time for the 1st Marine Division, now under the command of Maj. Gen. Herman Nickerson Jr. In Quang Nam Province, the four-day Operation Tuscaloosa finished on 24 January with 79 enemy dead and 17 weapons captured at a cost of 17 Marines killed and 52 wounded. Following the 1967 Campaign Plan, the Marines began replacing ARVN units at isolated outposts and assumed control of their TAORs, many of which had not been patrolled too vigorously in the past. This allowed the ARVN to redeploy for their new responsibilities of pacification, now grandly termed Revolutionary Development.

In the Duc Pho District of Quang Ngai Province, the 1st Marine Division conducted Operation Desoto in an area long dominated by the VC. Launched on 27 January, the operation involved two battalions, 3/5 and 3/7, clearing the VC along the axis of Highway One from Mo Duc, south of Quang Ngai city, to the boundary with Binh Dinh Province at the southernmost part of I CTZ. This was an important rice-growing and salt-producing area—both vital commodities in the Vietnamese diet—and therefore it was necessary to control their production and distribution while denying supplies to the enemy. Much of the countryside was waterlogged because of the northeast monsoon. This made progress extremely difficult, particularly the movement of supplies by truck. Marine ingenuity found a solution by stationing an LST laden with supplies off the coastline and using helicopters to bring them ashore as needed.

(A recurring task for the Marine Corps in I CTZ was to provide security to farmers during the harvest season so that the growers collected and retained their own produce while government forces could deny it to the VC/NVA. Such operations were termed Golden Fleece.)

The operation continued throughout February with extensive patrolling and the occasional fierce firefight such as the attack on the fortified village of Hai Mon that began in the early morning of 5 February with artillery, naval gunfire, and air bombardment to cover the helicopter insertion of 3/7 Marines. Companies L and M assaulted from an unexpected direction and soon entered the hamlets despite enemy automatic and recoilless-rifle fire. After further artillery and naval gunfire, the VC were forced to withdraw under fire from pursuing Marine riflemen, gunships, and fixed-wing aircraft. After the contact, the Marines discovered an extensive bunker and cave complex that combat engineers required some 3,600 pounds of explosives to destroy. Snipers remained a constant threat and the major cause of Marine casualties. Marine counter-sniper teams were deployed but the elusive enemy were difficult to pinpoint as most were single snipers firing from cleverly disguised "spider traps" that were only detectable from a distance of a few feet. Similarly, booby-traps were a frequent menace as Marines cleared and searched one anonymous "ville" after another, day after day. By the end of March, nearly all of the assigned area of operations had been cleared of the 95th VC Battalion and Operation Desoto ended on 7 April. Marine casualties were high, with 76 dead and 573 wounded. With some 21 square miles of Duc Pho District now returned to government control, the Marines handed the area over to the ARVN and its new Revolutionary Development teams. As they moved out, many Marines wondered when they would be back to clear the area of VC once more.

March 1967 was a significant month for the Marine Corps as the new M16 5.56-mm assault rifle was first issued in significant numbers and, on 18 March, M/Sgt. Barbara J. Dulinsky arrived in Saigon for assignment to the MACV combat operations center to become the first woman Marine to serve in South Vietnam. MACV also decided to commit U.S. Army units of 1st Cavalry Division (Airmobile) to I CTZ to allow the Marine Corps to concentrate its efforts in the three northern provinces and regain the initiative from the enemy. This was believed to be necessary because NVA pressure was growing along the DMZ, and the move also conformed to General Westmoreland's wish to expand Marine operations into the hinterland around the growing Khe Sanh combat base. In mid-April, General Westmoreland told the

The Thousand Yard Stare—fatigue and strain are etched on the face of Sgt. Small of 1st Platoon, Company F, 2nd Battalion, 7th Marines, among the sand dunes in the coastal area of Quang Ngai Province during heavy fighting in Operation Desoto on 6 March 1967.

An M60 team of Company B, 1/7 Marines, moves off on 13 March 1968 during Operation Worth, 15 miles southwest of Da Nang in Quang Nam Province. At 23 pounds, the M60 was a bulky and heavy weapon, that gave rise to its nickname of "Pig," whereas the communist equivalent, the Soviet RPD, weighed half as much.

Lance Cpl. E. F. Martinez cleans his M16 rifle during Operation Arizona south of Dia Loc on 18 June 1967. The new lightweight M16 assault rifle was first issued to the Marine Corps in February 1967. Problems soon arose in the field that caused the weapon to jam resulting in the deaths of troops in combat. The rifle's failings had a serious effect on morale and resulted in a Congressional inquiry. The problems were exacerbated by the belief among troops that the rifle did not require regular cleaning. The Force Logistic Command devised a modification program to rectify the shortcomings that continued throughout 1967, but a complete solution was not found until the introduction of the M16A1 in the following year. In the meantime, Marines were ordered to test-fire their rifles as they left on patrol. This they dutifully did with the unfortunate results that ammunition supplies were significantly depleted and Marines became conditioned to firing without aiming. Accordingly, the standard of marksmanship in combat declined sharply. Eventually the defects were eradicated and strict maintenance procedures were implemented to minimize problems in the field.

press: "We'll just go on bleeding them until Hanoi wakes up to the fact that they have bled the country to the point of national disaster for generations." His words echoed almost exactly those expressed by his opposite number, General Giap: "We will entice the Americans close to the border and bleed them without mercy."

On 20 April, U.S. Army Task Force Oregon established its headquarters at Chu Lai and came under the operational control of III MAF to reinforce the Marines in I CTZ. Four days later the bloody "Hill Fights" began on the Khe Sanh plateau. In extremely bitter fighting with North Vietnamese troops, units of the 3rd Marine Division cleared Hills 881S, 881N, and 861 overlooking the combat base. At the same time the enemy cut Route 9 to prevent reinforcements reaching the Khe Sanh area, except by air, as well as attacking Marine bases in Leatherneck Square. General Westmoreland's strategy was taking shape; so was General Giap's. Farther south below the border between Quang Nam and Quang Tin Provinces near Tam Ky, the 1st Marine Division was continuing its long-running vendetta with the 2nd NVA Division in the Que Son Valley, also known as Nui Loc Son Basin. The area had already seen heavy action, notably during Operation Harvest Moon in December 1965 and again during Operation Colorado in August 1966. A single rifle company was dispatched into the valley—"to create a situation" as the planning of HQ 1st Marines stated—in order to provoke the NVA to attack it whereupon elements of 3/1 and 1/1 would be flown in to engage the enemy in decisive battle.

Acting as the bait, Company F of 2/1 Marines set out in the early morning on 21 April and soon encountered small bands of NVA. Resistance grew as the company assaulted the hamlet of Binh Son 1. In

the opening intense volley of automatic weapons, small arms, and mortar fire from the well-entrenched NVA, 14 Marines were killed and 18 wounded with many of the latter collapsed on the open paddy field as the remainder of the Marines crouched behind the low paddy dikes or sought shelter in a nearby trench line. In an act of extraordinary courage, 18-year old Pfc. Gary W. Martini rushed forward to aid his stricken comrades, as his Medal of Honor citation records:

> In the face of imminent danger, Private Martini crawled over the dike to a forward open area within 15 meters of the enemy position where, continuously exposed to hostile fire, he hurled a hand grenade, killing several of the enemy. Crawling back through the intense fire, he rejoined his platoon which had moved to the relative safety of a trench line. From this position he observed several of his wounded comrades laying helpless in the fire-swept paddy. Although he knew that one man had been killed attempting to assist the wounded, Private Martini raced through the open area and dragged a comrade back to a friendly position. In spite of a serious wound received during this first daring rescue, he again braved the unrelenting fury of the enemy fire to aid another companion lying wounded only 20 meters in front of the enemy trench line. As he reached the

In a long and frustrating war, one of the only enduring certainties for the troops on the ground was that every effort would be made to evacuate a wounded soldier or Marine to a medical facility as quickly as possible. Injured troops were often evacuated by helicopter within 30 minutes of being hit and were on the operating table within 60. This had a significant bearing on survival rates as well as morale.

fallen Marine, he received a mortal wound, but disregarding his own condition, he began to drag the Marine toward his platoon's position. Observing men from his unit attempting to leave the security of their position to aid him, concerned only for their safety, he called to them to remain under cover, and through a final supreme effort, moved his injured comrade to where he could be pulled to safety, before he fell, succumbing to his wounds . . . His outstanding courage, valiant fighting spirit, and selfless devotion to duty reflected the highest credit upon himself, the Marine Corps, and the United States Naval Service.

A CH-53A Sea Stallion of Marine Heavy Helicopter Squadron 463 lands with supplies for the 105-mm howitzers of 11th Marines following heavy ammunition expenditure on the opening day of Operation Cochise, 11 August 1967, when over 1,000 rounds were fired in support of Marine units. Shown to advantage is the horizontal sliding-wedge breechblock and the hydropneumatic recoil system above the gun barrel. The first detachment of four Sea Stallions of HMH-463 arrived at Marble Mountain Air Facility on 31 December 1966. The Sea Stallions greatly increased Marine lift capabilities as they replaced the elderly piston-powered CH-37 Mojave helicopters.

With the bait taken at such cost, HQ 1st Marines declared Operation Union under way and dispatched Companies I and M of 3/1 in an air assault to support Company F. They were followed by 1/1 and the guns of Battery B/11, as the battle grew in intensity, while the 1st Aircraft Wing provided air support. At the same time, three battalions

Perched on the bow of an LVTP-5A1, a Marine engages a target on the shoreline with a Browning M1919A4 machine gun on 29 May 1967. The M1919 Browning was immensely reliable and better suited than the M60 to the saltwater environment in which the LVTP-5 operated.

of the 1st ARVN Ranger Group deployed to act as a blocking force in an operation they designated Lien Ket 102. The enemy in Binh Son 1 were routed and pursued for several days under a deluge of supporting fires that inflicted serious casualties. On 25 April, Operation Union passed to 5th Marines and 3/5 joined the fray while 1st Marines returned to the Da Nang TAOR but not the unfortunate F, 2/1. Fierce fighting continued and on 27 April the enemy exacted a heavy price when a Marine stepped on a mine that triggered a series of booby-traps on a helicopter LZ. One Marine was killed outright and 43 wounded of whom 35 required evacuation.

Operation Union continued into May with 1/5 Marines attacking enemy positions on Hill 110 in the mountains east of Hiep Duc supported by 1/3 Marines. In the ensuing day-long battle on 10 May, another tragedy occurred when four Marine F-4 Phantoms mistook A Company, 1/5, for the enemy and struck their position with eight rockets that killed five Marines and wounded another 24. Eventually the enemy were forced off Hill 110, leaving 116 bodies, but the Marines suffered 33 dead and 135 wounded. For the next five days the Marines had repeated contacts with the enemy until the operation was closed down on 16 May. The month-long battle resulted in 865 enemy dead, including 486 regulars of the 2nd NVA Division, with another 777 "probables," as well as taking 173 prisoners and 70 weapons. The cost to the Marines was 110 killed, 2 MIA, and 473 wounded, an ironic death toll after the tragic battle of Hill 110.

Within days, intelligence reports suggested that the 3rd and 21st NVA Regiments were returning to the area. The Marine response was Operation Union II. It began on 26 May with an air assault by 3/5

Lance Cpl. P.F. Blose of Golf Company, 2/1 Marines, engages floating debris with his M16 rifle in case it is an explosive device intended to destroy the Tu Cau bridge he is guarding during the fourth phase of Operation Pipestone Canyon in September 1969. Of particular note, he has a Three Pocket Grenade Carrier suspended from the equipment hooks of his late pattern M1955 fragmentation vest. The grenade carrier was particular to the Marine Corps and held up to six M26A1 fragmentation grenades.

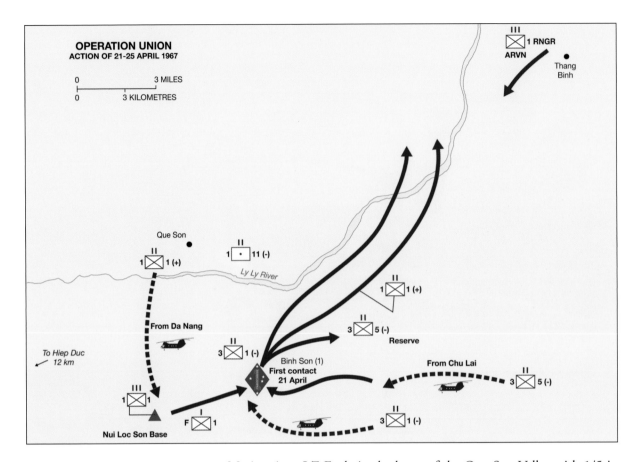

OPERATION UNION
ACTION OF 21-25 APRIL 1967

Operation Union was a major search and destroy mission against the 2nd NVA Division conducted in the Que Son Valley by the 1st and 5th Marines between 21 April and 16 May 1967.

Marines into LZ Eagle in the heart of the Que Son Valley with 1/5 in blocking positions at the western end of the valley. Unfortunately, it was a "hot LZ." L and M Companies came under intense fire as they landed. Within minutes one CH-46 Sea Knight was shot out of the sky. However, in a battle lasting throughout the day, the Marines overran the enemy bunker system, killing 118 NVA at a cost of 38 Marines dead and 82 wounded or one Marine casualty for every NVA body; this was not the kill ratio that General Westmoreland had ordained would achieve victory in a war of attrition. Over the next few days, contact with the enemy was sporadic until both Marine battalions, after air assaults into LZ Robin and LZ Blue Jay, returned to the area of the previous contact at LZ Eagle in a wide outflanking maneuver. Their target was the village of Vinh Huy designated Objective Foxtrot.

The attack began on 2 June and immediately ran into heavy resistance from 200 NVA dug in to the east of Vinh Huy. Fierce fighting raged for the next four hours until the Marines of 3/5 overran the position, although a helicopter then took a direct hit from a 57-mm recoilless rifle, killing one Marine and wounding seven others. Meanwhile, 1/5 had moved up to envelop Objective Foxtrot with Company D on the right and an attached company, F 2/5, on the left. To do so they had to cross a 1,000-yard-wide rice paddy facing a

horseshoe-shaped hedgerow. When halfway across, the Marines were caught in a withering crossfire. Company F was particularly hard hit in a scenario that was startlingly reminiscent of Company F, 2/1, during Operation Union I. With wounded and dead scattering the paddy field, the company commander, Capt. James A. Graham, called in an artillery

A "blooperman" of 1/7 Marines reloads his M79 grenade launcher during an assault under the covering fire of an LVTH-6A1 of the 1st Provisional Armored Amphibian Tractor Platoon during Operation Arizona in June 1967. The LVTH-6 was the fire-support version of the LVTP-5, armed with a 105-mm howitzer. Although always vulnerable to mines, these vehicles proved particularly useful over inundated ground that was impassable to conventional tanks.

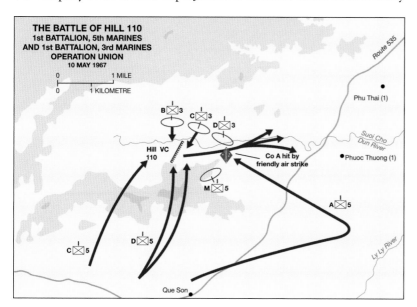

The Battle for Hill 110 was a fierce encounter between 1/5 Marines and the NVA on May 10 1967 during Operation Union.

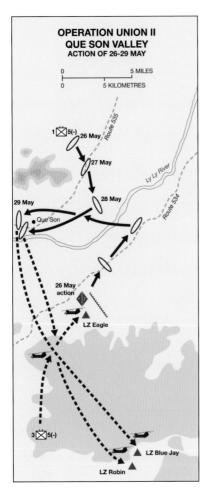

**OPERATION UNION II
QUE SON VALLEY
ACTION OF 26-29 MAY**

Air assault by helicopters proved fundamental during Operations Union and Union II in the pursuit of the elusive enemy.

bombardment on the hedgerow. His 2nd Platoon was pinned down completely by two concealed machine guns and unable to move or retrieve their wounded. When the artillery barrage stopped, Graham organized his company headquarters group and charged through his 2nd Platoon and silenced one of the machine guns, allowing some of 2nd Platoon to withdraw with the wounded. The small headquarters group held their ground under heavy fire as they tried to subdue the second machine gun. Graham was wounded twice during the fighting and personally killed 15 of the enemy, but the second enemy position kept up a sustained volume of fire. Graham therefore ordered his men to retire under his covering fire. Even when they reached a secure area, he refused to withdraw but chose to remain with one Marine who was too badly injured to be moved. His last radio transmission reported that an enemy force of 25 was attacking him. He died protecting the Marine he refused to abandon. Capt. James Graham was awarded a posthumous Medal of Honor.

With both battalions heavily engaged, the division reserve, 2/5 Marines, was committed to the battle by air assault. In the growing darkness, the reinforcements clashed with an NVA force trying to withdraw northwards. In the running contact, 2/5 suffered 20 casualties but they were fortuitously evacuated by a passing CH-53, though not before the helicopter was damaged by mortar and automatic-weapons fire on the emergency landing zone, returning to Da Nang with 58 holes in its fuselage. The sudden appearance of these timely reinforcements caused the NVA to abandon their fighting positions and withdraw to the southwest. The 1st Marine Aircraft Wing was ready for them. Using an unprecedented and unusual technique, two F-4 Phantoms attacked the fleeing enemy. The first flew low and slow with its landing lights on to attract enemy small-arms fire while the second followed shortly behind without running lights and unleashed napalm on the hapless NVA firing into the sky.

With the departure of the enemy, the 5th Marines regrouped for the night and evacuated the wounded. On the following day, all three battalions policed the battlefield. The Marines counted 476 enemy dead around the contested paddy field and hedgerow. The Marines lost 71 killed and 139 wounded. During a sweep of the area for the fallen, the Marines encountered some NVA engaged on collecting their own dead. Neither side opened fire. In a tacit agreement, an undeclared truce lasted all day as the bodies of each side were retrieved, including that of Capt. Graham.

Operation Union II closed on 5 June 1967 with another 110 Marines killed in action but the 5th Marines were subsequently awarded a Presidential Unit Citation for their achievements in Operations Union I and Union II. The Que Son Valley remained a

matter of unfinished business for the 1st Marine Division. In the same month of June there were some significant command changes within III MAF with the departure of Lt. Gen. "Uncle Lew" Walt and his replacement by Lt. Gen. Robert E. Cushman Jr. The commander of the 1st Marine Division, Maj. Gen. Herman Nickerson Jr., now became Deputy Commander III MAF, and the division passed to Maj. Gen. Donn J. Robertson. Divisional operations against the 2nd NVA Division and the 1st VC Regiment in the Que Son Valley and its environs continued throughout the summer with two battalions of 5th Marines on almost constant patrol in the area as well as conducting Operation Adair in late June, Operation Calhoun in July, Operation Cochise in August, and Operation Swift in September. Throughout, the fighting was fierce and sustained, with heavy casualties on all sides.

Operation Swift was notable for further heroic actions that led to the award of two Medals of Honor. On the opening day of the operation, 4 September 1967, Companies B and D of 1/5 Marines were heavily engaged by enemy forces near the hamlet of Dong Son 2. Two UH-34 helicopters of HMM-363 were hit trying to evacuate the casualties and one was shot down. A UH-1E of VMO-2, callsign "Deadlock," was also shot down and crash-landed inside the Company D perimeter, whereupon its radio callsign became "Deadlock on the deck." The pilot, Maj. David L. Ross, continued to direct air strikes throughout the

Pfc. D.A. Crum of Hotel Company, 2/5 Marines, has his wounds treated by Corpsman D. R. Howe during the street fighting in Hue City. Universally known as "Doc," the U.S. Navy corpsmen attached to every Marine unit in South Vietnam gained legendary status for the selfless care they gave to the wounded while taking appalling risks to retrieve the injured on the battlefield.

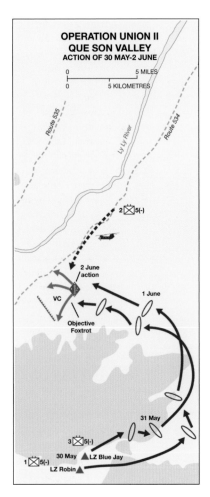

OPERATION UNION II
QUE SON VALLEY
ACTION OF 30 MAY–2 JUNE

Operations Union and Union II saw the award of several Medals of Honor to members of the 1st Marine Division.

There were more than enough hazards in the field besides the enemy—wild animals such as tigers or water buffalo, snakes and spiders, ferocious ants and bees, tropical sores and malaria, let alone mines and booby-traps. Life in the field was dirty and dangerous but for every combat rifleman dozing fitfully in a foxhole at night, there were four or five soldiers or Marines who slept between sheets on comfortable cots, often in air-conditioned huts, in relatively secure base camps; they were known as REMFs by combat troops.

action while the machine guns and ammunition from his aircraft were used to bolster the perimeter defenses.

Companies K and M, 3/5 Marines, were flown in by helicopter as reinforcements to a position northeast of the contact; on board one of the helicopters was the chaplain of the 3rd Battalion, 5th Marines, Lt. Vincent R. Capodanno USN. As they advanced across open paddy fields, the 1st and 2nd Platoons of Mike Company were caught in a classic L-shaped ambush and struck by intense mortar, machine-gun, and small-arms fire from an entrenched enemy force. While the 1st Platoon was able to withdraw to a small knoll, the 2nd Platoon under Sgt. Lawrence D. Peters was pinned down and unable to maneuver. The remainder of Company M rallied on the 1st Platoon position, soon to be called the "Grassy Knoll." The enemy quickly encircled the Marines and pounded them with mortar bombs and automatic-weapons fire.

Meanwhile, the 2nd Platoon was attempting to withdraw to the knoll, but without success due to the weight of fire from the hidden enemy positions. Disregarding his own safety entirely, Sgt. Peters stood up to attract the enemy fire and point out their firing positions from the muzzle flashes until he was shot in the leg. Throughout the hot, dusty afternoon, Peters ignored his painful wound as he directed his squad but was injured again in the face and neck by an exploding mortar round. Standing erect once again, Sgt. Peters fired burst after controlled burst at the enemy until he was critically hurt by a gunshot wound to the chest. Although unable to stand or move, he steadfastly continued to direct the firepower of his Marines until they gained fire superiority and were able to carry the assault to the enemy. Only then did Sgt. Peters succumb to his wounds.

Throughout this fierce and relentless action the 2nd Platoon was comforted and inspired by the presence of their chaplain. When

In a squad-level contact between US infantry and the NVA/VC Main Force units, their respective firepower was evenly matched despite the common perception that the US armed forces enjoyed overwhelming superiority. At the close range of most firefights, all the weapons used were more than accurate enough. The communist AK47 Kalashnikov assault rifle was extremely rugged, reliable and easy to maintain in the field. The same could not be said for the M16 rifle. With a cyclic rate of 550 rounds per minute, the M60 machine gun was much heavier than its Degtyarev RPD opponent. Both sides made extensive use of hand grenades, the communists making many of theirs from unexploded American artillery shells and bombs. For destroying targets at greater distances such as bunkers, the Americans used the M79 grenade launcher or the M20 rocket launcher, later replaced by the M72 LAW, whereas the communists made effective use of the RPG (both the RPG-2 and RPG-7) as both a direct- and indirect-fire weapon. These were also used against American AFVs and helicopters with devastating effect. American Marines and soldiers had considerable respect for their enemy's weapons and small-unit tactics. Here, an M60 team returns fire during Operation New Castle on 26 March 1967. Shown to advantage is the personal weapon of an M60 gunner with a .45-caliber M1911A1 Colt automatic pistol in a black leather holster at his hip. Typically, this gunner and assistant of Company F, 2/5 Marines, are festooned with 200-round belts of 7.62-mm ammunition.

company headquarters learnt that the 2nd Platoon was in danger of being overrun by a massed enemy assault, Lt. Capodanno left the relative safety of the Grassy Knoll and sprinted unarmed across open fire-swept ground to join the 2nd Platoon as they battled for their lives. With total disregard for his own safety in the vicious fusillade, Capadanno moved around the battlefield administering last rites to the dying and giving medical aid to the wounded, some of whom he manhandled up the slope of the Grassy Knoll to the less-exposed Company M position. When he returned to the 2nd Platoon, a mortar round exploded nearby inflicting multiple fragmentation wounds to his arms and legs while his right hand was almost severed. Despite the pain of his injuries, he refused medical treatment and directed the Navy corpsmen to help the fighting Marines instead of himself. Undaunted, he continued to move about the battlefield encouraging and exhorting "his Marines" by word and deed. Father Vincent then saw a Navy corpsman struck down as he tended to a wounded Marine just 15 yards from an enemy machine-gun position. Capadanno dragged himself forward to assist "Doc" Leal but as he reached the mortally-wounded corpsman he too was cut down by machine-gun fire and the two Navy non-combatants died together.

Artillery and air strikes continued to pound the enemy positions long into that bloody afternoon. As darkness fell, an A-6 Intruder placed a well-aimed bomb on a key enemy emplacement on nearby Hill 63 and the heavy fighting gradually subsided. On the following morning, the Marines policed the battlefield to find 130 dead NVA soldiers as against their own casualties of 54 killed and 104 wounded. Both Sgt. Peters and Lt. Capodanno were posthumously awarded the Medal of Honor. The death of Lt. Capodanno hit the Marines hard, as this letter by Marine Jack Swann attests:

Operation Swift was another major
search and destroy mission conducted
by the 1st Marine Division in the Que
Son Valley during September 1967. It
also resulted in the award of two Medals
of Honor.

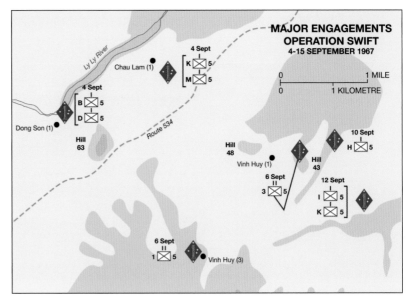

I was at that time a lance corporal walking point for the 1st
Squad of 1st Platoon, Mike Company, 3/5 Marines, when the
NVA opened up on us that afternoon. I knew Capodanno was
with our company. When I got back to a bomb crater up the
small hill later that night, a wounded Marine told me
Capodanno was one of the KIAs wrapped in a poncho along
with the other Marines who died that day. Early the next
morning, I listened to the wounded and the still-walking talk
about how Capodanno gave up his life to help the fallen
wounded, bringing them to safe cover, and giving last rites to
the men who were dying in the field of fire. Father Capodanno
cared more about the men he was with than he did his own life
that day, and I honor him for that. I also learned that next
morning that my friend Doc Leal was dead. They were both
killed together. Capodanno giving last rites to a wounded
Marine from 2nd Platoon and Doc Leal trying to patch the
Marine up. Great men from Mike Company died that day.
They all deserve the highest honors. *Semper Fi.*

Father Vincent Capodanno was indeed an extraordinary man who
garnered enormous respect; one corporal of 3/5 Marines summed it up
with the words: "Somehow he just seemed to act the way a man of God
should act." He was known during his service with the Marine Corps as
"The Grunts' Padre" as he is to this day. Such is his fame that on 21 May
2006, 39 years after his death in the Que Son Valley, Capodanno was
publicly declared Servant of God by the Roman Catholic church in the
first step towards canonization. In the best Navy tradition, the *Knox*
Class frigate, FF-1093, was named USS *Capodanno* in memory of "The
Grunts' Padre."

The importance of a chaplain to the fighting men in any military unit is often overlooked as their spiritual welfare is fundamental to good morale as is the role of the Navy corpsman. Attached to every Marine platoon, the corpsman gave immediate first aid to the injured on the battlefield, stabilized their wounds, and organized their evacuation for further medical treatment. Universally known as "Doc," he provided the day-to-day medical care for Marines, treating cuts and bruises or blisters as well as undertaking such mundane tasks as distributing anti-malaria pills or prophylactics for Marines going "downtown." The corpsman was also a vital component of the pacification program when

Holding his M1911A1 pistol aloft, Pfc. Roger D. Jenkins of Company G, 2/1 Marines, wades through a rice field during a search and clear mission seven miles east of the An Hoa Combat Base on 21 July 1969 as part of Operation Pipestone Canyon. While the M1955 fragmentation vest was mandatory on operations, it proved almost impossible to persuade Marines to zip up the vest thus the vulnerable thoraco-abdominal area of the body remained unprotected.

Grasping on to liana vines, Marines of Delta Company, 1/5 Marines, climb through difficult terrain during Operation Cochise on 17 August 1967. "Wait-a-minute" vines were one of innumerable impediments to mobility in the field.

Men of Company E, 2/7 Marines, race across rice fields under heavy fire during Operation Arizona on 20 June 1967. A smoke round lands as a ranging marker before supporting artillery engages the enemy in the treeline, a scenario repeated thousands of time in South Vietnam.

he provided "Medcap" to Vietnamese villagers for a whole host of ailments and diseases. Festooned with all sorts of bandoleers and pouches filled with medical supplies and carrying extra water bottles to succor the wounded, the corpsman's primary tool was his "unit one medic bag" containing all manner of medical paraphernalia to save the lives of his Marine comrades. Many corpsmen did not carry weapons as the weight of pistol or rifle and ammunition meant that less medical equipment could be carried. Their casualty rate in battle was horrendous and of the 15 U.S. Navy Medal of Honor recipients during the Vietnam War four were corpsmen.

The actions during Operations Union and Swift epitomized the problems facing U.S. forces in South Vietnam. Each invariably began with a well-coordinated ambush by NVA or VC forces against a small American unit, usually of platoon size. These attacks were based on regular and timely intelligence of American troop movements. The ambushes were triggered from temporary spider holes that were nigh on impossible to detect except at close quarters, or from well-constructed bunkers. The latter could be prepared months in advance and used only when necessary. The bunkers were well stocked with ammunition for prolonged contacts should the force commander wish and were strong enough to withstand bombardment from most weapons except a direct hit from aerial bombs, heavy artillery, or tank cannon fire, a luxury denied to most allied troops in contact with the enemy. In the initial exchange of fire, the Americans frequently suffered casualties necessitating swift treatment and evacuation. This compromised immediate offensive action against the enemy as fire support from various agencies was coordinated to cover the withdrawal of the wounded and to fix the enemy in place. The enemy was only too well aware of the American propensity to come to the aid of the fallen. They had no compunction in shooting Navy corpsmen or those trying to assist the wounded lying in open ground.

In response, and with considerable skill, officers and senior NCOs quickly implemented sophisticated fire plans against an entrenched enemy, using tube artillery from nearby fire support bases, naval ships offshore, helicopter gunships, or ground-attack aircraft. These included such types as the heavily armed and armored A-1 Skyraider and "fast movers" in the close air support role such as the dependable A-4 Skyhawk, the versatile F-4 Phantom II fighter/bomber, the cannon-armed F-8 Crusader fighter, or the all-weather A-6 Intruder attack aircraft. All had different flight characteristics and carried different types of ordnance that had to be taken into account in any coordinated fire plan. Such plans therefore took time to put in place. This often gave the enemy a range of opportunities: to leave the battlefield, having inflicted debilitating casualties upon the Americans; to adopt what was termed "hugging" tactics whereby they got so close to the Americans that any fire support could not be used against them for fear of striking friendly

The inevitable cost of war as dead Marines, still clutching their rifles, await removal from the battlefield following a firefight. The brutal fighting in Vietnam resulted in a greater number of Marine casualties than World War 2.

Company E, 2/7 Marines, moves through heavy brush during Operation Arizona on 20 June 1967. For an M60 team laden down with spare ammunition, such terrain was particularly punishing. The towel around the neck helped to prevent the bullets from chafing as well as cushioning the weight of the M60 on the shoulder.

Under the supporting fire of an LVTP-5A1 amtrac, Marines of 2/5 assault a Viet Cong position during Operation New Castle on 26 March 1967. Strapped to the haversack of the Marine in the foreground is an M1943 "E-tool"; the entrenching tool was a vital item of Marine combat equipment and served a host of purposes beyond its basic function of digging foxholes.

forces; or to continue the fight from their heavily fortified and well disguised bunkers that were impervious to all but the heaviest of weapons.

But this brief generalized summary of the mechanics of small-unit actions fought throughout South Vietnam gives little inkling of the brutal reality of war faced by the grunt on the ground as he humped through the boonies towards yet another dusty ville under the broiling sun. Corporal Andrew Garner of 2nd Platoon, Company K, 3/7

A gun crew prepare their M19 60-mm mortar for firing. The 60-mm mortar provided fast and responsive firepower to a rifle company with three such weapons in the mortar section.
Each mortar squad comprised a squad leader, gunner, assistant gunner and three ammunition carriers, each with approximately 12 mortar bombs.
The M49A2 HE round weighed 3.07 pounds and could be fired out to 2,000 yards but 1,000 was the optimum range for accuracy with an effective bursting radius of almost 20 yards.

Marines, recalls one such patrol near Chu Lai in 1967. His account graphically highlights the problems of identifying friend from foe and innocent from deadly threat; the need for constant vigilance even when hungry and thirsty and laden down with 60 pounds of equipment; and the fatal price of making a mistake in Vietnam:

We were patrolling through a village that we patrolled just about every day. I was walking point and this was one time that I let my guard down. Upon entering the village, I saw some soldiers but I thought that they were ARVN. The village did not show any signs of the enemy. About halfway through the village a nine-year-old girl came from behind a hootch with a grenade in each hand, heading straight for me. I did not have time to try to stop her. Through experience and my quick reaction, I shot this child. The two grenades went off and wounded two of my men. At this point, all hell broke loose. We were surrounded in the village and the VC were letting us have everything they had. They didn't care who they killed—they were after us. We knew that we had only one chance for some of us to make it and that was for us to try and break through their lines. That was a mistake because on our way out we tripped two booby-traps, killing six Marines and wounding 14. That stopped our assault and we took cover where we could fire. The firefight lasted for three hours before help came. Even today I think that if I just followed my instinct then, some of these men would still be alive. I think a lot of the child I had to kill. There's not a day that goes by that I do not think about this experience, especially since I have a little girl of my own.

Special Landing Force: Keeping the Faith

THE SPECIAL LANDING FORCE (SLF) was the floating strategic reserve of the U.S. Navy Pacific Command for all of Southeast Asia and not just South Vietnam. The SLF usually comprised a battalion landing team (BLT) of a Marine infantry battalion with artillery, armor, amtrac, and logistical support to allow independent operations on land. Helicopters, amtracs, and landing craft were the principal means of transporting the Marines to shore. Many of these elements were drawn from formations deployed to South Vietnam—which naturally wished to retain control of units employed by the SLF rather than reduce their strengths in-country. The SLF, however, was under the operational control of the U.S. Seventh Fleet and the 9th Marine Amphibious Brigade based at Okinawa while at sea, but was available for use by MACV and III MAF in South Vietnam. Once the SLF had landed, it then came under the command of the higher land formation or the SLF commander himself if acting independently, but only once control had been relinquished by the naval commander. At that point logistical support passed to III MAF or MACV depending on its geographical deployment. This was a recipe for confusion in command and control. It was for this reason that SLF operations were almost exclusively conducted in I CTZ. The SLF was carried by the Amphibious Ready Group of the U.S. Navy comprising up to five LSTs, an amphibious assault ship (LPH), a dock landing ship (LSD), an attack transport

The successor to the famous LVTs of World War 2 was the LVTP-5 family that entered service from 1956. The standard troop carrier in Vietnam was the LVTP-5A1, shown here conducting an operation along the coast with the Special Landing Force. The vehicle had a capacity for 34 Marines or 45 if all standing in an emergency. It could carry 5,443 kg of cargo and the standard armament was a single .50-caliber Browning machine gun in a simple cupola.

As the war in I CTZ turned into a prolonged land campaign, the LVTP-5 amtrac was increasingly employed in the APC role to transport Marines on operations. However, the vehicle was highly vulnerable to mines because there were 12 fuel cells located along the belly of the hull that invariably caught fire following a mine explosion. Accordingly, troops preferred to travel on the top of the amtrac where they would be blown off the vehicle with a greater chance of survival. Due to an anomaly of deployment in March 1965, the 1st Amphibian Tractor Battalion was attached to the 3rd Marine Division and the 3rd Amtracs to the 1st Marine Division.

(APA), and an amphibious transport dock (LPD). In 1967, a second SLF was created and both were now committed to extended operations in South Vietnam, acting as a rapid reaction force for reinforcing III MAF forces in-country.

A typical SLF operation was Deckhouse VI, undertaken in February 1967 in support of the 7th Marines conducting Operation Desoto. The opening phase began on 16 February with landings from helicopters and amtracs near Tach By that were unopposed since the enemy had fled. Several days before MACV had published a Notice to Airmen that informed commercial aircraft to avoid the area; the VC were therefore given timely intelligence of the planned landing. Supporting fires for the assault landings were compromised because of the U.S. Army Task Force X-Ray operating to the south and the 7th Marines to the north while Vietnamese villagers congregated on a ridgeline to watch the Marines landing. Once on land the Marines met only desultory VC sniper fire and the troops re-embarked on 26 February. On the following day, SLF helicopters landed at LZ Bat where eight of the 14 aircraft were hit by enemy fire and six put out of action. After repeated air strikes, the VC withdrew and Phase II of Operation Deckhouse VI became a repeat of Phase I with only intermittent contact and sniper fire over the next six days. The SLF operation claimed 279 enemy dead as against 12 Marines killed in action. Operation Deckhouse VI ended on 3 March 1967 and the SLF sailed for the Philippines.

Between 1965 and 1969, the USMC conducted 62 amphibious operations. These actually achieved very little in terms of enemy casualties but were highly important in maintaining and refining amphibious warfare doctrine in a testing combat environment. The SLF combination of infantry, armor, amtracs, helicopters, and supporting arms was a valid military exercise for the U.S. Marine Corps in the absence of a coherent overall military strategy in South Vietnam.

OPPOSITE: With the strain of combat etched on his face, Lance Cpl. C.D. Bradford clutches a Thompson sub-machine gun in his wounded hand as Charlie Company, 2/5 Marines, clear buildings in the New City of Hue on 5 February 1968. With its heavy .45-inch caliber, the M1A1 was a most suitable weapon for street-fighting but must have been difficult to come by even in the arcane Marine Corps supply system. The radio handset indicates that he is a radio telephone operator while the "Claymore bag" carried spare batteries and parts for the AN/PRC-25 FM radio.

The Tet Offensive

At a speech at the National Press Club in Washington, DC, on 21 September 1967, General Westmoreland declared publicly: "We have reached an important point where the end begins to come into view . . . I am absolutely certain that whereas in 1965 the enemy was winning, today he is certainly losing." A recent MACV statistical analysis had declared that the war had reached the fabled "crossover point" in Westmoreland's strategy of attrition whereby the enemy's battlefield losses exceeded his ability to replace them. However, his year of the big battles had not brought the expected decisive encounters with the enemy on the battlefield during major operations such as Junction City and Cedar Falls. The Rolling Thunder bombing campaign against North Vietnam had failed to produce the anticipated results with little diminution of Hanoi's ability to wage war in the South. The year had ended in military stalemate, a situation that favored Hanoi's strategy of protracted guerrilla warfare. It is one of the awful ironies of the Vietnam War that the only "crossover point" reached at this stage in 1967 was in the U.S. opinion polls when for the first time ever, more Americans (46 percent) disapproved of the war than supported it (44 percent). In reality, Hanoi was willing to send many more men to the slaughter as the Tet Offensive and the siege of Khe Sanh were to prove.

Nevertheless, both MACV and Washington exuded optimism, giving the impression to an increasingly skeptical American public that the war was being successfully prosecuted after so long and at such cost in blood and treasure. But General Giap had persuaded the Hanoi leadership that now was the time for a general offensive in South Vietnam, spearheaded by the NLF, against provincial capitals and cities across the country, with the NVA deployed in support. Fundamental to his strategy in I CTZ was the siege of Khe Sanh combat base. As Giap wrote: "More and more American units had to be moved into the battle zone, drawing them away from the task of gaining control of the rural population." By the beginning of 1968 Giap was able to claim: "The Marines are being stretched as taut as a bowstring."

At the start of 1968, III MAF had a strength of 81,115 including 77,679 Marines and 3,436 sailors, a net increase for the year of 10,737. There were now 21 Marine infantry battalions in I CTZ together with 31 ARVN, 15 U.S. Army, and four Republic of Korea Marine battalions. Of the Marine Corps' total strength of 298,498, 81,249 were now in South Vietnam: 21 out of 36 ground battalions, 14 out of 33 fixed-wing squadrons, and 13 out of 24 helicopter squadrons. The Marine Corps units were now concentrated in the three most northerly provinces with the bulk of its forces, 12 infantry battalions, stretched along the "McNamara Line" below the DMZ. With the 1st Marines at Quang Tri City under the operational control of the 3rd Marine

Men of 2/5 Marines rush forward to their next objective under the covering guns of an M48A3 Patton tank. At the outset of the Tet Offensive, the 3rd Tank Battalion was in the process of deploying from Phu Bai to Quang Tri. En route to the LCU ramp at Hue, the last four tanks, two M48A3 and two M67A2 flame tanks of the H & S Company, were diverted to support 2/5 Marines. They gave invaluable fire support throughout the battle for Hue City.

Division, the 1st Marine Division had its two remaining infantry regiments, 5th and 7th, deployed to Thua Thien Province as part of Operation Checkers, the northward movement of all Marine units towards the DMZ. Marine casualties for the year 1967 were 3,452 killed and 25,994 wounded compared to enemy losses estimated to be 25,452 dead and 23,363 as probably killed. It marked another crossover point as the Marine Corps had now suffered more casualties in Vietnam since the first losses in 1962 than in the Korean War; the total now stood at 5,479 dead and 37,748 wounded. And the worst was yet to come.

General Westmoreland was convinced that the siege of Khe Sanh was to be the decisive battle of the war, on a par with the decisive battle of Dien Bien Phu of 1954 that saw the end of French colonialism in Indochina. Both MACV and the White House became obsessed with this isolated outpost near the Laotian border. Reinforcements poured northwards. By mid-January, almost 50 maneuver battalions or one-half of all U.S. combat troops were concentrated in I CTZ. Westmoreland's and Giap's strategies had meshed perfectly. On 20 January 1968, the 77-day battle of Khe Sanh began. It was the apotheosis of each opposing general's style of warfare: Westmoreland's prodigious employment of firepower and Giap's prodigal expenditure of manpower. Yet Giap had another card to play. With the approach of the lunar New Year or Tet that is traditionally the most important Vietnamese holiday, a truce was declared so that families could be reunited to celebrate the week-long festivities. With many ARVN soldiers on leave and all American eyes riveted on Khe Sanh, South Vietnam lay vulnerable to attack.

During the vicious street fighting in Hue, the Marines made extensive use of CS gas to flush the enemy out of buildings, hence these Marines of 2/5 Marines are wearing their M18 protective masks during an attack on 6 February 1968.

Marines of 3rd Platoon, Hotel Company, 2/5 Marines, carry a wounded comrade to cover during street fighting in Hue City on 6 February 1968.

Soon after midnight on 30 January, after weeks of covert infiltration, over 80,000 VC and NVA soldiers launched a widespread series of assaults across every military region of South Vietnam. All the major cities and 36 of the 44 provincial capitals were attacked, as well as other high-profile targets. In I CTZ these included concerted rocket bombardments of all the Marine air bases to neutralize allied tactical air support in the region, but the prime target was the old imperial capital city of Hue. Within hours 7,500 VC and NVA troops (4th and 6th NVA Regiments with the 12th NVA Sapper Battalion, plus local VC units) had occupied Hue and gained all their objectives, except for the MACV compound close to the Perfume River and the headquarters of the 1st ARVN Division in the northeast corner of the walled Old City with its historic and symbolic Imperial Palace. Once they had consolidated their positions, the VC cadres began the systematic massacre of some 3,000 professional people in Hue and the slaughter of hundreds of others who were marked down for execution as supporters of the Saigon government, designated as "cruel tyrants and reactionary elements." Such killings were standard practice when VC/NVA forces overran government-controlled hamlets and villages, the only difference was the scale when transposed to a city.

The Tet Offensive achieved almost total tactical surprise despite a mass of intelligence data that had been accumulated by MACV. With the battle of Khe Sanh raging, any captured documents outlining the overall

With his M2 .50-caliber machine gun at hand, the commander of a Late Model M48A3 scans the upper stories of buildings for enemy RPG teams during the fighting in Hue City on 2 February 1968 in support of Company F, 2/5 Marines. Note the bullet damage to the optics of the vision block ring of the commander's M19 cupola.

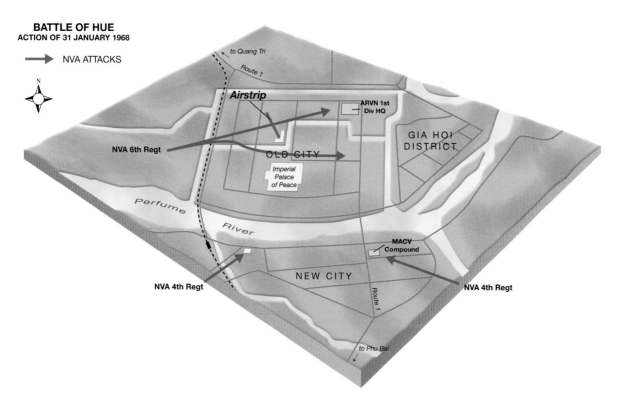

BATTLE OF HUE
ACTION OF 31 JANUARY 1968

→ NVA ATTACKS

N

to Quang Tri

Route 1

Airstrip

ARVN 1st
Div HQ

GIA HOI
DISTRICT

NVA 6th Regt

OLD CITY

Imperial
Palace
of Peace

Perfume

River

MACV
Compound

NVA 4th Regt

NEW CITY

Route 1

NVA 4th Regt

to Phu Bai

Assault routes of the NVA during the initial attack on Hue City and the Citadel.

Tet plan were seen as disinformation. As one of Westmoreland's intelligence officers admitted: "Even if had I known exactly what was to take place, it was so preposterous that I probably would have been unable to sell it to anybody." Despite dreadful confusion, the 1st Marine Division was quick to react. The nearest units were at Phu Bai, eight miles to the south, as part of Task Force X-Ray, comprising HQ elements of 1st and 5th Marines and three understrength infantry battalions, 1/1, 1/5, and 2/5, refitting after weeks of heavy combat. There was to be no respite. In the early morning of 31 January, Company A, 1/1 Marines, was dispatched by truck up Route 1 towards Hue. On the way it met up with a platoon of M48 tanks and they joined forces but were stopped soon after crossing the Phu Cam Canal into the city by the K4C NVA Battalion in a fierce firefight. Task Force X-Ray dispatched reinforcements with Golf Company, 2/5, and the command group of 1st Marines. The combined force then fought its way against fierce resistance to the MACV compound, arriving around 1500 hours.

Out of touch with events on the ground and the scale of the enemy incursion, III MAF ordered Company G, 2/5, to advance across the Perfume River into the enemy-held Old City. Company G suffered severe casualties as it crossed the river and, once at the Thuong Tu Gate into the Citadel, it was met by a hail of fire from numerous concealed positions bordering the long, straight streets and hidden in the narrow bisecting roads. The situation was dire and it took two hours for the

Marines of Company A, 1/1 Marines, lower a wounded comrade from the rooftop of one of the buildings of the Hue University on 2 February 1968. Street fighting is always costly in casualties and Hue City was no exception.

Men of 2/5 Marines lay down a base of fire as other Marines maneuver against enemy positions. After its troublesome introduction into service, the M16 proved to be an effective personal weapon during the Vietnam War although some Marines preferred the heavier caliber M14 7.62-mm rifle to the end.

Marines to withdraw to the MACV compound. They had incurred 33 percent casualties out of a strength of 150. It was a portent of things to come. More Marine reinforcements arrived with Foxtrot and Hotel Companies joining Golf in Hue. Meanwhile, ARVN forces were trying to recapture the Old City. To simplify command and control, the ARVN was made responsible for operations north of the Perfume River in the Old City and the Marines to its south in the New City, while U.S. Army units sealed off the city to the west. At the start, heavy weapons were forbidden so as to preserve the historic buildings of Hue but once the scale of the NVA occupation was realized such restrictions were eased. However, the weather was consistently bad, with constant rain or drizzle and low cloud cover that precluded close air support. In the vicious street fighting that characterized the battle of Hue City, the

Marines employed every sort of infantry weapon at their disposal and a host of armored fighting vehicles (AFVs)—M48 Patton tanks, M67 flamethrower tanks, M50 Ontos self-propelled 106-mm recoilless rifle anti-tank vehicles, and M42 Duster self-propelled 40-mm anti-aircraft guns—as direct fire support weapons.

From the outset, both MACV and the South Vietnamese tried to downplay the scale of the communist occupation of Hue. It was a bad miscalculation. This attempt at news management did a total disservice to the Marines fighting one of the bitterest battles of the war and it was shown to be a lie as television images of the fierce fighting flickered through the living rooms of millions of Americans. To the grunts on the ground such matters were meaningless. Tasked with evicting the enemy from the New City, the Marines methodically began house clearing—room by room, floor by floor, building by building, street by street, and block by block—in the most ferocious urban warfare the Marine Corps had endured since Inchon and Seoul in Korea in 1950. As always, urban warfare was one of the most difficult of all military operations and one of the most expensive in casualties. It was to last for 26 days.

Typical of the fighting was the action on 4 February of the 3rd Platoon of Company A, 1/1 Marines—the first Marine unit sent into Hue. The 3rd Platoon had been led by Sgt. Alfredo Gonzalez after the platoon commander was wounded during fighting around Con Thien in December 1967. Just 21 years old, Gonzalez was on his second tour of duty in South Vietnam but he seemed older and more mature than his contemporaries. Lieutenant Ray L. Smith took command of Company A after Capt. Gordon D. Batcheller was wounded on the approaches to the MACV compound in Hue and recalls:

Marines of Hotel Company, 2/5 Marines, enjoy a light moment of relief as Gunnery Sgt. F.A. Thomas maneuvers a child's pedal car during the battle for Hue City on 4 February 1968. Note the two patterns of helmet covers with the "gunny" displaying the standard "leaf pattern" and the Marine behind the Korean War vintage "duck hunter" version.

> The thing that probably is most surprising and maybe says a lot about him is that I thought of Sergeant Gonzalez as an old veteran. At the time, I remember thinking of him as an old-timer, a guy who had been around a while. I was just 21 and as it turned out he was four or five months younger than me. I remember him as a real mature, grown-up sergeant type of a guy, as opposed to the 21-year-old that he was. He was a real quiet person, but he always had a smile on his face. He was a little restrained in his emotions, but that was probably because he was truly one of the "grown-ups" in our organization . . . Like a lot of people that you remember for their actions, my memory of him is as a big muscular guy. He was actually fairly small. I'm 6 feet 2 inches tall and 218 pounds. Recently a friend sent me a photo of Sergeant Gonzalez and I standing beside each other. I couldn't believe I was that much bigger than him. It was just the opposite in my memory. He was the big one.

An M40A1 106-mm recoilless rifle team of 2/5 Marines prepare their weapon for firing in a classroom of Hue University on 3 February 1968. In the words of one of the gunners: "We fired it with a lanyard where we knocked out our objective—we kind of knocked out the building that the 106 was in too, but it didn't hurt the gun, once we dug it out." Readily visible above the 106 is the .50-caliber spotting rifle that acted as a ranging device. With near-identical ballistics to the 106, the tracer round of the spotting rifle created a burst of smoke on striking the target. The recoilless rifle was then fired to hit the same spot. Ordinarily, the trigger was pushed forward to fire the spotting rifle and pulled to fire the 106.

(Ray "E-Tool" Smith became a major general and the commandant of Camp Lejeune until his retirement from the USMC. He got his nickname after attacking an NVA machine-gun position with an entrenching tool when his M16 rifle jammed during the battle of Hue City. As a military analyst, General Smith accompanied 1/7 Marines of the 1st Marine Division in the advance on Baghdad in 2003 during Operation Iraqi Freedom.)

Gonzalez was wounded during the action at the same time as Capt. Batcheller was shot. Gonzalez then single-handedly destroyed a

Snipers are a potent weapon in urban warfare and they claimed many victims on both sides during the battle of Hue City with the communists using the elderly Moisin Nagant Model 1891/30 equipped with a telescopic sight as opposed to the Marine M40 and Redfield sight. Here, Lance Cpl. Gene Davis of Company D, 1/5 Marines, engages a target with the latter during the fighting in the Citadel in the final days of the ferocious battle.

machine-gun bunker with hand grenades before rescuing a wounded Marine under fire. Despite his own injuries, he refused to be evacuated. Over the next few days, despite being wounded again on 3 February, he led his platoon with heroism and fortitude while at all times ensuring his men suffered as few casualties as possible. During a company assault against the Jeanne d'Arc Girls High School, the attack faltered under withering fire from a well-entrenched NVA force. Typically, the NVA employed machine guns at ground level to provide a high volume of grazing fire along streets while snipers and RPG teams roamed the upper floors of buildings to fire down on advancing Marines, while pre-registered mortars bombarded all likely avenues of approach, which were booby-trapped as well. Against such concerted opposition, progress was slow, dangerous, and exhausting in the bone-chilling rain.

Adorned in a black beret, Sergeant Reginald Hiscks fires his M3A1 "Grease Gun" during fighting with Company A, 1/1 Marines, in the Citadel on 20 February 1968. Strapped to his back is a bandoleer with four extra clips of .45-caliber ammunition. The M3A1 was the standard weapon of Marine AFV crewmen. He is also armed with a .45-caliber M1911A1 pistol in a shoulder holster, suggesting he is a crewman from an Ontos or M48 Patton tank.

The school and its attached church were a key objective and, like most buildings in Hue, stoutly constructed with an open courtyard in the middle and scores of windows to act as firing points for snipers and RPG teams. Smith recalls: "We were trying to secure the church and the enemy was inside the school. We had to blow holes in the walls so we could get through and take the schoolrooms. It was very tough fighting." The Marines found the venerable 3.5-inch rocket launcher to be a highly effective tool to create man-sized holes in building walls or else a block of C-4 plastic explosive acted just as well at close quarters. With one wing of the school captured, RPG teams firing from across the courtyard halted further progress. Sgt. Gonzalez grabbed several M72 LAWs (Light Anti-Armor Weapon) and climbed to the second floor where he played a deadly game of hide and seek. Appearing at a window, he waited until an NVA gunman revealed himself and then engaged the position with a 66-mm HEAT round. Eventually his luck

An exhausted crewman of an M50A1 of the 1st Anti-Tank Battalion attached to the 1st Tank Battalion catches some much-needed sleep during the battle of Hue City in February 1968. Despite its light armor, the Ontos proved highly effective during the savage street fighting, often working in pairs with an M48 tank as a "killer team" with rifle squads. Firing a combination of HEAT and HEP rounds, the 106-mm recoilless rifles provided accurate and destructive direct fire support against fortified positions while Beehive rounds were devastating in the anti-personnel role and to screen troop movements in the heavily contested streets. The Ontos unit employed during Operation Hue City was Company A (Minus) comprising the 3rd Platoon and a heavy section of the 1st Platoon, making a total of eight vehicles.

ran out and he was struck in the midriff by a B-40 rocket and fell mortally wounded. Sergeant Alfredo Gonzalez was awarded the only Medal of Honor given during the battle of Hue City. In 1995, he became the first Mexican-American to have a modern warship named after him when the *Arleigh Burke* Class destroyer DDG-66 was launched, an appropriate pennant number for a Marine who died wielding a 66-mm rocket launcher.

It is intriguing to speculate whether Sgt. Gonzalez would have survived had the full gamut of Marine fire support been available to Alpha Company. On the day after his death, warships were allowed to provide supporting fire and on 7 February artillery and close air support was added. The nature of the fighting changed dramatically. By 9 February, the New City was cleared of the enemy. Two days later, the 1st Battalion, 5th Marines, entered the Old City in force following insertion by helicopter and landing craft along the Perfume River. There the bloody battle continued in support of the 1st ARVN Division. The street fighting was savage and unremitting. The enemy were pounded unmercifully with 5,191 naval rounds, 18,091 artillery shells, and 290,877 pounds of aerial ordnance, as well as Marine direct-fire weapons. Of these, the M48 Patton and the M50 Ontos proved particularly effective despite the received wisdom that AFVs were a liability in urban warfare. The 90-mm main armament of the Patton was devastating against NVA bunkers and fortified positions while the smaller Ontos was able to provide valuable fire support even in the narrow streets. With its six 106-mm recoilless rifles, the Ontos was used to engage all manner of targets from sniper holes to heavy doorways. Though it had often been criticized for its revealing backblast on firing, the Marines now used the clouds of dust it created to mask their dashes across fire-swept roads. Similarly, a 106-mm "beehive" flechette round fired into the plaster wall of an enemy-held building formed an improvised smoke screen to aid fire and movement. The tanks received multiple hits from B-40 rockets but they kept fighting, although their crews were exchanged some five or six times. Marine scout–sniper teams waged their own deadly form of individual warfare against the numerous NVA snipers who were burrowed into the very fabric of the city.

In its first assault on 12 February beside the northeast wall of the Citadel, Company A, 1/5 Marines, lost two killed and 30 wounded with virtually the whole command group among the casualties, resulting in it being forced to withdraw to reorganize. Bravo and Charlie Companies joined the fray. Used to operating in the boonies as they were, the built-up city of Hue came as a nasty and dreadful baptism in urban warfare for 1/5 but they were quick learners. One major concern was the problem of orientation in the maze of streets due to a lack of military maps so local Texaco gas stations were raided for every street

A Marine of Company H, 2/5 Marines, carries an elderly woman patient from the city hospital to relative safety during the heavy fighting in the New City of Hue. As with all urban warfare, the greatest victims were the civilians, suffering a tragic loss of life as well as the destruction of their homes and livelihoods.

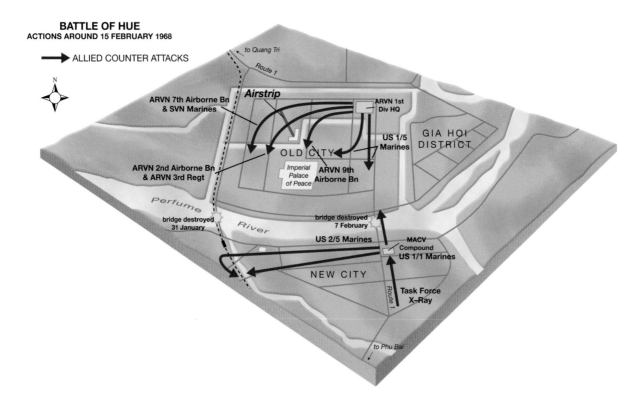

BATTLE OF HUE
ACTIONS AROUND 15 FEBRUARY 1968

➡ ALLIED COUNTER ATTACKS

N

to Quang Tri

Route 1

Airstrip

ARVN 7th Airborne Bn
& SVN Marines

ARVN 1st
Div HQ

GIA HOI
DISTRICT

US 1/5
Marines

OLD CITY

Imperial
Palace
of Peace

ARVN 9th
Airborne Bn

ARVN 2nd Airborne Bn
& ARVN 3rd Regt

Perfume

bridge destroyed
31 January

River

bridge destroyed
7 February

US 2/5 Marines

MACV
Compound
US 1/1 Marines

NEW CITY

Route 1

Task Force
X–Ray

to Phu Bai

ABOVE: Assault routes of the Marines during the recapture of Hue City and the Citadel.

RIGHT: Combat engineers of the 1st Engineer Battalion fire in support of Marine units during the fighting in Hue City. The combat engineers undertook many tasks to assist the advance of the infantry by destroying enemy bunkers or blowing holes through walls.

plan to be had. In five days of vicious street fighting, 1/5 Marines suffered 47 killed and 300 wounded or one casualty for every yard of ground gained. Replacements were fed into the meat grinder direct off the flights from the United States. Many of them were killed in the same fatigues and boots as they had worn in Camp Pendleton; worse, some died without anyone in the unit ever knowing their names. After the first week, only two of the ten rifle platoons had officers in command:

sergeants or even corporals led the remainder. On 22 February, the battalion gained its final objective—the Thuong Tu Gate where three weeks earlier Company G, 2/5, had suffered such heavy casualties on the opening day of the battle for the city. On the same night, the enemy withdrew from Hue leaving just a diehard rearguard. On 24 February, the huge NLF flag that had flown above the Citadel throughout the battle was finally hauled down. Marine casualties were 147 killed and 857 seriously wounded. The 1st Marines were awarded a Presidential Unit Citation for having "soundly defeated a numerically superior enemy force . . . by their effective teamwork, aggressive fighting spirit, and individual acts of heroism and daring." Hue City was added as yet another battle streamer to the colors of the 1st Marine Division.

From Khe Sanh to Keystone

The Tet Offensive had failed. For Hanoi it was a significant military defeat. For the NLF it was a disaster. The communists suffered almost 50,000 dead—more than the total number of Americans killed in action throughout the Vietnam War. The NLF was destroyed as a political entity. Its infrastructure of local cadres was severely damaged everywhere in South Vietnam. Henceforth, the military and political

Deep in the heart of the Royal City of Hue, Sgt. P. L. Thompson of 1/5 Marines poses with his M14 rifle on the throne of the Emperor Tu Duc in the Imperial Palace of Perfect Peace on 24 February 1967 at the conclusion of the battle of Hue City. As its name implied, the palace was declared a strict no-fire zone in the midst of one of the fiercest battles of the Vietnam War and fortunately suffered only minor damage.

In pouring rain, Lance Cpl. Ronald J. Casey, a squad leader with the 2nd Platoon, Company G, 2/7 Marines, returns fire in a firefight on 26 November 1968 during Operation Meade River. To ward off the elements, he is wearing a Parka, Wet Weather (a U.S. Navy issue item) over which he has an M1955 flak vest and rucksack. By this time, the modified M16A1 rifle that overcame the problems of the earlier models was now in widespread service and thereafter the M16 proved to be an effective weapon in the difficult combat conditions of the Vietnam War.

direction of the war was to be controlled exclusively by Hanoi and so, in terms of *realpolitik*, this was a satisfactory outcome for the politburo, despite the vast expenditure of blood. For General Westmoreland, it was the long-sought victory on the battlefield, although not at a time or a place of his choosing. Now was the time to strike back at the enemy when they were on the ropes. MACV dusted off the contingency plans for attacking the enemy sanctuaries in Cambodia, Laos, and across the DMZ. Now was the time to unleash the bombers against the restricted targets in Hanoi and the port of Haiphong. The battle plans were in place. General Westmoreland just needed another 200,000 troops. The final decision lay with Washington. Overwhelmed by media hysteria and failing health, President Lyndon Johnson demurred. Bui Diem, the South Vietnamese ambassador to the United States, was a shrewd observer of the Washington scene:

> Not long after, it became clear to me that the complete withdrawal of U.S. forces from Vietnam would be only a matter of time and modalities. In that sense, the Tet attacks of 1968 could well be considered a prelude to the end of the war five years later. Thus Tet was the climax of the Second Indochina War. Indeed, to me, Tet was the time when U.S. public opinion and misconception snatched defeat from the jaws of potential victory.

General Westmoreland was relieved of his command. President Johnson announced that he would not stand for re-election. The Commander-in-Chief had given up the will to fight in South Vietnam and, with him, so had the body politic in Washington. It was left to the troops in the field to carry on the battle. As General Giap later stated: "We were not strong enough to drive out a half-million American troops, but that wasn't our aim. Our intention was to break the will of the American government to continue the war."

Throughout February and March, the battle of Khe Sanh raged on. Far from turning into another Dien Bien Phu as many had feared, American airpower and the skill at arms of the 26th Marines achieved a further victory at a cost of 205 American deaths with an estimated enemy toll of 10,000. The siege ended in April as the battered remnants of the enemy slipped away into their jungle sanctuaries in Laos. On 4 April, U.S. troop levels in South Vietnam reached their highest with 545,000 men in-country, of whom 85,966 were Marines with 85,402 in III MAF. This was more than one-quarter of the entire Marine Corps and more Marines than went ashore at Iwo Jima or Okinawa. As commander of III MAF, General Cushman now had more troops under his control in I CTZ (24 Marine and 28 U.S. Army battalions) than any other Marine in history. During February and the height of the Tet Offensive, the Marine Corps suffered the highest casualty rate of the

Stretcherbearers of Company C, 1/7 Marines, rush a wounded Marine to a waiting CH-46 helicopter for aeromedical evacuation to a field hospital following a booby-trap explosion at the conclusion of Operation Scout in February 1968. The rapid evacuation of casualties by helicopter was one of most positive aspects of the Vietnam War and significantly reduced the fatality rate of combat wounds.

An M60 team covers the advance of Mike Company, 3/7 Marines, during a sweep through the hamlet of Chau Son II, ten miles south of the city of Da Nang on 20 November 1968. Searching the "rocket belt" around the Da Nang airbase was a repeated task for the 1st Marine Division. Soviet-supplied 122-mm free-flight rockets were a constant menace to the aircraft and personnel stationed at the airbase. Simple to construct and conceal, rocket launch sites were extremely difficult to detect and any Marine lucky enough to find one was given six days R & R in-country, later improved to leave in Australia, Thailand, or Hong Kong, such was the importance of protecting Marine air assets.

war with a total of 4,891 (including 691 KIA and 4,197 WIA), but the highest monthly death toll of the war occurred in May with 810 KIA—almost exactly the same number of Marine dead as in the first four years of warfare in Iraq. This reflected the continuing scale of operations in I CTZ particularly in the 1st Marine Division TAOR.

While media attention was concentrated on Saigon and Hue during the Tet Offensive, the 1st Marine Division thwarted a major attack by the 2nd NVA Division on Da Nang through air strikes, artillery, and the judicious deployment of 3/5 Marines. Continual pressure was exerted on the enemy south of Da Nang by 1st and 2nd Battalions, 7th Marines, during Operation Worth in March. In May, the 7th Marines pursued the enemy through their safe haven of Go Noi Island in Operation Allen Brooke. This was followed by Operation Mameluke Thrust, lasting into July in an area known as Happy Valley to the southwest of Da Nang. Meanwhile, the 5th Marines continued operations in the An Hoa TAOR. In early September, the 1st Marines, until then operating along the DMZ with the 3rd Marine Division, returned to divisional control

in the Da Nang TAOR. In October, Operation Maui Peak was mounted to destroy enemy forces investing a Green Beret Special Forces camp at Thuong Duc in central Quang Nam Province.

Much to the consternation and confusion of the American public, the Khe Sanh combat base was razed to the ground and evacuated by 5 July 1968. Territory deemed to be vital just six months before was now abandoned, as were the fixed defenses of Leatherneck Square below the DMZ. Both the 1st and 3rd Marine Divisions adopted more mobile operations. At the same time, the command structure in I CTZ was changed to reflect the growing U.S. Army presence in the region. With almost five divisions in the northern provinces, a Provisional Corps was created and on 15 August this became the XXIV Corps, an historic U.S. Army designation. While XXIV Corps was subordinate to III MAF, the 1st Marine Air Wing was now placed under the control of the Seventh U.S. Air Force for all operations in Vietnam, both South and North. A fundamental aspect of Marine independence was being eroded. Again, it meant little to the grunts on the ground. For them the war dragged on unabated. As of 13 June 1968, Vietnam became America's longest war.

The protracted Operation Mameluke Thrust, conducted by the 1st Marine Division since 18 May, ended on 23 October with 2,728 enemy claimed dead as against Marine casualties of 267 dead and 1,730 wounded. It was immediately followed by Operation Henderson Hill. In November, an Accelerated Pacification Program known as Le Loi was implemented by the South Vietnamese government. This was intended to restore control over the rural hamlets and villages lost during the upheavals of the Tet Offensive in February and "Mini-Tet" in May. In support of Le Loi, the 1st Marine Division mounted Operation Meade River—the largest Marine airmobile operation of the war. It was designed to trap three NVA regiments—the 36th, 38th, and 368B—in an area known as "Dodge City" some 15 miles south of Da Nang. The Marines often named enemy base areas and "free fire zones" after Wild West locations such as "Dodge" City and the "Arizona Territory" as any man found there was deemed to be a "gunfighter" and therefore fair game in combat.

In just two hours, 76 helicopters flew 3,500 Marines into 47 different landing zones, while scores of trucks transported ARVN and Korean soldiers into position to create a 25-mile cordon of 7,000 allied troops. This represented a three-man fire team every 20 yards. The operation came under the command of 1st Marines and included 1/1, 2/5 and 3/5 Battalions. As the cordon contracted so contacts with the enemy increased until the operation was declared over on 9 December by when 841 NVA/VC had been killed and 182 captured. The Marines lost 107 dead and 385 wounded. Farther west in the "Arizona Territory," Operation Taylor Common opened on 7 December

Displaying a certain cultural insensitivity, two Marines pose with "Miss Arizona" in the "Arizona Territory" while wearing the most popular "soft covers" in the heat of Vietnam. On the left is the standard Marine Corps Utility Cap with the "eagle, globe and anchor" badge and on the right a locally produced short brimmed "boonie" hat in ERDL camouflage pattern as are the combat pants. The four-colour camouflage was developed in 1948 by the U.S. Army's Engineer Research and Development Laboratories hence ERDL. The camouflage uniform was styled identically to the third pattern tropical combat uniform.

conducted by 5th Marines and BLT 2/7. This was to continue well into 1969. And so 1968 closed as it had started with Marines fighting across I CTZ. It had been the bloodiest year of the war.

During the year, the Marine Corps lost 5,063 dead (including 26 MIA) and 29,320 wounded—more than one-third of the casualties during the entire war. In an appalling catalogue of attrition, the 1st Marine Division averaged about 120 dead and 1,000 wounded a month as against 80 and 700 respectively in the 3rd Marine Division, giving a lie to the belief that the counterinsurgency campaign conducted by the 1st Marine Division was less dangerous than the conventional warfare along the DMZ. At the same time, the two divisions killed on average 1,500 enemy a week during the first six months of the year. Of particular note, the nature of the casualties in the two divisions also differed markedly. In the 3rd Marine Division, mortars and artillery weapons caused 47 percent of casualties while mines and booby-traps inflicted 18.2 percent. In the 1st Marine Division, the reverse applied with 17.9 percent due to indirect fire and 50.8 percent to mines and booby-traps. The remainder of the casualties were caused by small-arms fire. Combat riflemen accounted for 80 percent of the casualties with privates, privates first class, and lance corporals accounting for 75

Marines of Golf Company, 2/5 Marines, attack a machine-gun position on Go Noi island during Operation Allen Brooke on 7 May 1968. The Marine in the foreground is laden down with an AN/PRC-25 radio whereas the others have dispensed with their rucksacks for the assault.

A gun crew of the 4th Battalion, 11th Marines, fire an M114A1 155-mm howitzer in support of 2/5 Marines during Operation Taylor Common near An Hoa, 25 miles southwest of Da Nang, on 5 January 1969. A full gun crew for the M114 comprised 11 men and the weapon fired a 95-pound projectile to a range of 16,350 yards; this was some 3,000 yards greater than the 105-mm howitzer and more importantly its shells were almost three times as heavy for much greater terminal effect. With a weight of 12,950 pounds, it was possible for a medium-lift helicopter to carry the M114 as an under-slung load. This allowed the M114 to be emplaced in the far-flung fire support bases across the divisional TAOR. Just prior to the Vietnam War, the Marine Corps replaced its M114 towed howitzer with the M109 self-propelled howitzer in divisional artillery regiments to increase mobility. As more and more fire support bases were established so the requirement grew for more artillery weapons. The old M114 towed howitzers were taken out of storage and shipped to South Vietnam. Ironically, as the M114 was air-transportable by helicopter, it proved to have much greater tactical mobility than the self-propelled howitzers that, being essentially road-bound, were confined to major combat bases as "fortress artillery."

percent of the casualties. Their average age was just under 20 years and 6 months. In September, the troop strength of III MAF reached its peak at 85,520 Marines but by the end of the year the Marine component had dropped to 81,000. The U.S. withdrawal from South Vietnam had begun.

In January 1969, Richard M. Nixon was inaugurated as the 37th President of the United States. He had been elected on a pledge to achieve "peace with honor." The principal plank of the new administration's policy was "Vietnamization" whereby the ARVN was to be expanded and equipped to undertake the bulk of the ground fighting. The new MACV commander, General Creighton W. Abrams, promulgated his "One-War" strategy, which demanded more mobile and flexible tactics and an end to the "body count" war of attrition. Smaller units now conducted "clear and hold" operations instead of "search and destroy." Pacification was now a priority. Most U.S. forces were to be concentrated around important strategic cities and areas while the ARVN conducted the ground war with lavish fire support provided by U.S. airpower and artillery bases. For many Vietnam old hands in the Marine Corps, it was what they had advocated all along. For the 1st Marine Division, its primary mission became the defense of Da Nang and its environs. In effect, the Marines were returning to their enclaves of 1965. The concomitant of Vietnamization was the phased withdrawal of U.S. forces following the opening of "peace negotiations" in Paris on 10 May 1968. In III MAF, the redeployment of troops was

Pfc. George W. Barber of 2nd Platoon, Golf Company, 2/7 Marines, opens up with his M60 machine gun on a suspected Viet Cong position during Operation Meade River about three miles southeast of Hill 55 on 26 November 1968; Hill 55 was the home of the 1st Marine Division sniper school. On his left hip, Barber has an "assault pack" of 100 rounds of 7.62-mm ammunition issued in a waxed cardboard box carried in a cotton bandoleer.

known as Operation Keystone and the first phase, Keystone Eagle, began on 1 July 1969 with the initial elements of the 3rd Marine Division leaving South Vietnam for Okinawa. By the end of the year, the complete division had departed.

For the enemy, 1968 was a cataclysmic year. The Tet Offensive did not succeed militarily. The hoped-for spontaneous uprising of the South Vietnamese people failed to materialize. The NLF was broken and its infrastructure badly damaged. A last throw of the military dice in May, known as "Mini-Tet," had resulted in another costly defeat. Casualties during these full-scale offensives were appalling even by Hanoi's casual standards of bloodletting. And yet. In this curious new world of rapid communications, the politburo was fully aware of events in America as race riots, assassinations, student radicalism, and government duplicity tore the country apart. They saw the respected CBS anchorman, Walter Cronkite, declare on primetime television:

Wearing M1955 body armor, the veteran journalist Walter Cronkite conducts an interview with Lt. Col. Marcus J. Gravel of 1/1 Marines during a visit to I CTZ in February 1968. On his return to the US, Cronkite made a dramatic broadcast on the CBS Evening News declaring that the war was unwinnable. President Johnson admitted that "If I've lost Walter, I've lost Middle America." To many observers and historians, it was a turning point in the war.

For it seems now more certain than ever that the bloody experience of Vietnam is to end in a stalemate ... it is increasingly clear to this reporter that the only rational way out then will be to negotiate, not as victors, but as an honorable people who lived up to their pledge to defend democracy, and did the best they could.

Then they knew they had time on their side. When they were able to take propaganda photographs of a famous American film actress sitting astride an anti-aircraft gun in Hanoi, they knew they were fighting a country at war with itself. For Giap, it was vindication enough for the failures of 1968, as he claimed of the Americans: "Until Tet they had thought they could win the war but now they knew they could not." Hanoi returned to the strategy of "protracted war" but with the new political lever of "protracted peace negotiations."

Virtually all the commanders of III MAF were veterans of the Korean War. They were only too aware of the new reality that came with the Paris peace negotiations. More U.S. casualties were incurred during the Korean War after peace talks began at Panmunjom than in the fighting before them. And so it happened in the Vietnam War. Similarly, the problems of maintaining morale once peace negotiations were under way became paramount—who wanted to be the last soldier to die on Pork Chop Hill, in the Iron Triangle, or in Dodge City? As troop levels fell in South Vietnam, so did morale. The Marine Corps was not immune from these problems as racial tension, drug abuse, and "fragging" proliferated ("fragging" was the attempted murder of officers and NCOs, often with fragmentation grenades hence the term; the 1st Marine Division recorded 47 such incidents with one dead and 47 injured). At the start of 1969, III MAF comprised 79,844 Marines, 3,378 Navy, and 59,403 U.S. Army soldiers; by the end, following

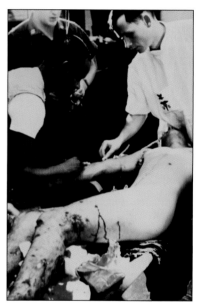

With extensive fragmentation wounds to the legs, a Marine is treated aboard the amphibious assault ship USS *Tripoli*. Medical advances and rapid aeromedical evacuation meant that the seriously wounded had a significantly greater survival rate than in previous wars. Mines and booby-traps were the primary cause of casualties in the 1st Marine Division for much of the war. More tellingly, 56 percent of frontline troops witnessed the death or wounding of their comrades in battle, a dreadful memory that lingers for many veterans to this day.

With a stack of rounds readily at hand between the split trails, an M101A1 105-mm howitzer of India Battery, 3rd Battalion, 11th Marines, undertakes a fire mission on 28 August 1969. A full gun crew of an M101A1 was eight men but crews were often undermanned leading to physical exhaustion during prolonged fire missions. One of the most common missions was termed H & I or harassment and interdiction whereby artillery weapons fired on particular targeted sites periodically so as to deny freedom of movement to the enemy. Unfortunately H & I missions were largely ineffectual yet consumed the greater proportion of all artillery shells expended in South Vietnam. The 105-mm barrel had a life expectancy of approximately 20,000 rounds before replacement was necessary.

further troop withdrawals, there were 54,541 Marines, 2,144 Navy, and 61,792 Army. In January 1970, further troop reductions were announced that affected the 1st Marine Division directly. It now lost most of its armor support with the departure of the 1st Anti-Tank Battalion and its Ontos vehicles; the 1st Tank Battalion (except one company of M48 tanks that was to remain in-country); and the 3rd Amphibian Tractor Battalion as its LVTP-5 amtracs were now near the end of their service lives.

With these USMC departures, there were now more U.S. Army personnel than Marines in I CTZ. Accordingly, on 9 March, XXIV Corps became the senior U.S. command in the region rather than III MAF. The 1st Marine Division was now the principal fighting arm of III MAF with some 21,000 men based around the 1st, 5th and 7th Marines, and the 11th as its artillery support. Operations in Quang Nam Province continued the while (*see map*). These included Operation Imperial Lake in the old stamping ground of the Que Son area. This turned out to be the last major Marine offensive of the war. It was also the last operation for the 7th Marines who began leaving South

Vietnam in September as did the last company of M48 tanks. The 5th Marines followed in February 1971. In 1970, the Marine Corps suffered 403 killed and 3,625 wounded as against 1,051 and 9,286 respectively in 1969.

Only the 1st Marines remained. Their principal task was patrolling the "rocket belt" to protect the Da Nang air base. On 14 April 1971, III Marine Amphibious Force stood down after almost six years in-country. On 30 April, President Nixon officially welcomed the 1st Marine Division home in a nationally televised ceremony. It was if the Marine Corps heaved a common sigh of relief; as General Cushman said: "We are pulling our heads out of the jungle and getting back into the amphibious business." In place of III MAF, the 3rd Marine Amphibious Brigade (3rd MAB) was activated on 1 March comprising some 13,600 Marines. This was based around the 1st Marines, a fixed-wing group MAG-11, a helicopter group MAG-16, and the 2nd Combined Action Group (the Marines maintaining their belief in pacification to the end), as well as logistical and medical support. It was to become operational on 14 April, the day III MAF stood down, but was overtaken by events.

C-34, an M48A3 of 3rd Platoon, Company C, 1st Tank Battalion, negotiates rough terrain in the Go Noi island area during Operation Pipestone Canyon on 2 June 1969. This was the largest operation conducted by the 1st Marine Division in 1969 and lasted from June until November. The 1st Tank Battalion provided close direct-fire support to the infantry and the 90-mm cannon of an M48 was always welcome to a Marine rifleman in contact.

Leading from the front, Lt. Col. Francis X. Quinn marches at the head of his men of 3/7 Marines during Operation Mameluke Thrust in September 1968 in support of an ARVN mission in the Dodge City sector. Close behind him is his RTO for immediate communications with his troops or higher formations.

The gun crew of an M101A1 105-mm howitzer of Battery G, 3rd Battalion, 11th Marines, shelter from the powerful downdraft of a CH-53A Sea Stallion on an ammunition resupply mission during Operation Pickens Forest to disrupt Base Area 112 of the 38th NVA Regiment and the 577th Rocket Battalion southwest of An Hoa on 18 July 1970. During the operation, Fire Support Bases Defiant, Mace and Dart were created to allow the 11th Marines to provide artillery coverage for the 7th Marines. The self-contained artillery fire support bases also acted as patrol bases for the infantry units and as the tactical headquarters for the command elements of any given operation. Artillery weapons were able to provide fire support irrespective of the weather and commonly had the first rounds on target within five minutes of a request from a unit in the field.

The next increment for departures under Operation Keystone was announced on 7 April with the troops to leave South Vietnam by 30 June. The 3rd MAB was to be among them with 1/1 Marines standing down on 13 April. Accordingly, the brigade lost a third of its fighting strength on the day before it became operational. Patrols continued in the Que Son area with Operation Imperial Lake until it was terminated on 7 May. Battery C, 1st Battalion, 11th Marines, had fired its last rounds in anger on the day before. During its five years in-country 1/11 Marines fired approximately 2.5 million artillery shells. On 7 May, 16 A-4 Skyhawks of VMA-311 flew their last bombing mission into Laos; the CH-46 Sea Knights of HMM-262 flew their last combat sorties and the last three companies of the Combined Action Program were deactivated. By 26 May, the last riflemen of 2/1 Marines were on their way home to Camp Pendleton in California.

The Vietnam War was the longest and in some ways the largest war in Marine Corps history. The USMC strength reached a peak of 317,400, as against 485,113 in World War 2. However, some 730,000 Marines served in the Corps during the six years of major American involvement in the Vietnam conflict (1965–71) as opposed to some 600,000 in World War 2. From 1 January 1961 to 9 December 1972, 12,963 Marines were killed in action—28.4 percent of the U.S. total—and a further 1,679 died of non-battle-related causes. A further 88,589 Marines were wounded in action but only 26 were taken prisoner while another 93 were missing in action. In World War 2, 19,733 Marines were killed and 67,207 wounded. To feed this mammoth military machine, the Marine Corps required some 9,000 to 10,000 replacements each month in the Far East with an annual turnover of up to 120,000. In all, some 500,000 Marines served in South Vietnam itself. Throughout their tour of duty, the vast majority of Marines served their country with honor and gallantry in a confusing and tragic crusade that cost millions of lives and ruined millions more.

In April 1975, the Marine Corps returned to South Vietnam to evacuate personnel as the country fell to the communists. In the final hours two Marines of the Embassy Security Guard, Cpl. Charles McMahon Jr. and Lance Cpl. Darwin J. Judge, were killed at Tan Son Nhut Air Base; Judge was just 19 years old. In the confusion, it proved impossible to retrieve their bodies. For the Marines, it was the worst possible way to leave the battlefields of Vietnam.

South Vietnamese civilians are evacuated in a CH-46A Sea Knight. The twin-rotor Boeing-Vertol CH-46 was the principal U.S. Marine Corps medium helicopter of the Vietnam War. It was used for all manner of tasks from air assault and medical evacuation to logistical support and vertical replenishment at sea. It entered service with the Marine Corps in 1964 and first saw action in South Vietnam during 1966. The last personnel of the U.S. Embassy in Saigon were evacuated by a CH-46 Sea Knight on 29 April 1975 at the conclusion of the helicopter war.

The Marines depart. Although the 1st Marine Division was welcomed home by President Nixon on 30 April 1971 the last elements of the division did not leave until the end of May. Marine Corps advisors continued to serve in South Vietnam thereafter and provided invaluable support during the NVA Easter Invasion of the northern provinces in April 1972. Following the release of American POWs by North Vietnam on 26 March 1973, the last American advisors left South Vietnam, although 159 Marines remained to guard the US Embassy in Saigon.

EQUIPMENT & UNIFORMS

LEFT: Rifleman, 7th Marines, Qui Nhon, 1965. On their arrival in South Vietnam in July 1965, the riflemen of 2nd Battalion, 7th Marines, were mostly outfitted in the recently introduced OG107 utility uniform, together with black leather combat boots. The primary infantry weapon was the 7.62-mm semi-automatic M14 Rifle. The M1 Steel Helmet was similar to the World War 2 version and featured a reversible Leaf Pattern Camouflage Cover. To carry his personal equipment, he has a plywood Packboard to which is attached an M1941 Haversack below which is a 200-round metal ammunition can to support the unit M60 machine gun. On the outside of the haversack is an M1943 Entrenching Tool with a Marine Jungle First Aid Kit below its handle. Wrapped around the haversack is a Tent Shelter Half and regulation blanket together with tent poles and pegs. His load bearing equipment is the M1961 Web Gear, comprising suspenders that are worn under the body armor, the rifle belt together with four ammunition pouches holding one 20-round 7.62-mm magazine each, and an M6 Bayonet in its M8A1 Scabbard. The body armor is the USMC M1955 "flak vest" with rope ridge on the right shoulder to keep the rifle in position when firing.

RIGHT: M60 Gunner, 5th Marines, Hue, 1968. The street-fighting during the battle of Hue in February 1968 was intense and unremitting while being fought in foul, cold, and rainy conditions. Warmth and protection against the wet were a prime concern and this Marine has acquired a U.S. Navy issue Parka – Wet Weather which is worn over the tropical combat uniform but beneath the M1955 Armor – Body Fragmentation Protective vest. The 7.62-mm M60 machine gun is slung across his shoulder with the integral bipod extended for instant use with 200 rounds of ammunition in disintegrating link belts draped around his torso. A further 100 rounds are carried in a waxed cardboard box hung in a cotton bandolier below which is the carrying bag for a M17 Chemical-Biological Field Mask since CS gas was widely used during the battle. In the elastic retaining band around the helmet is a plastic bottle of LSA – Lubricant Small Arms – and a tooth brush for cleaning the M60 machine gun, commonly known as the "Pig." He is also armed with a .45-caliber automatic pistol in a black leather M1916 holster attached to his M1961 belt.

LEFT: Marines clamber aboard a UH-34D with the man in the doorway "humping" the tube of an 81-mm mortar strapped to a World War 2 era Packboard that remained in service with the Marine Corps throughout the Vietnam War to carry bulky and heavy loads. The second Marine has the M1941 Haversack on his back worn as a light marching pack. Below it is a Korean War vintage Dispatch Bag which was commonly used by officers in the early days to carry maps, pens, notebooks, and similar items. The Marine Corps has traditionally retained useful items of equipment in service long after they have been superseded in other branches of the armed services, although this was sometimes by choice rather than by design due to lack of funding.

LEFT: Rifleman, 1st Marines, Arizona Territory, 1969. By 1969, the camouflage tropical combat uniform designated as Coat/Trousers, Man's, Camouflage Cotton, Wind Resistant Poplin, Class 2, was in widespread use in the Marine Corps. The ERDL four-color camouflage pattern quickly became popular leading to such unofficial items as the locally produced utility cap or "cover." This rifleman is wearing the late pattern M1955 "flak vest" with integral cargo pockets in the nylon cover. Slung over the shoulder is a Charge Assembly Demolitions Bag M183 or "demo bag" that carried all manner of items in the field such as extra ammunition and personal effects. On his M1961 belt he carries a jungle first aid kit, a K-Bar knife, two water canteens, two M1956 universal pouches (acquired from US Army or ARVN personnel), and M26A1 Fragmentation Grenades. Over his shoulder is the later 5.56mm M16A1 automatic rifle with "bird cage" flash suppressor. By 1969, the initial teething problems with the M16 had been overcome and it had gained full acceptance within the Marine Corps.

ABOVE RIGHT: Mines were the greatest hazard to AFVs in Vietnam and much engineer effort was expended to counter the menace. Here, a combat engineer employs a mine detector on the verges of Route 9 as an M48A3 (Mod B) advances cautiously behind. Standing in front of the tank in the bush hat is the acclaimed combat photographer, Dana Stone. He was subsequently killed by the Khmer Rouge in Cambodia in 1971. In the same year his younger brother Thomas joined the U.S. Army and served as a combat medic in the Vermont National Guard. He was killed by friendly fire in March 2006 during his third tour of duty in Afghanistan.

RIGHT: A Marine scout–sniper team demonstrates the standard equipment used in Vietnam of the Model 700 Remington that was adopted by the USMC on 7 April 1966 as the Rifle, 7.62-mm, Sniper M40. It was commonly fitted with the Redfield Accu-Range 3–9x variable power telescopic sight. Note the Redfield Supreme lens cover flipped open that provided a water- and dust-tight seal for the front objective lens of the telescopic sight. It is estimated that in Vietnam approximately 50,000 rounds of small arms ammunition were expended for every casualty inflicted. The snipers of the 1st Marine Division achieved a bullet to casualty ratio of just 1:3. During the war, a round of 7.62-mm ammunition cost 13 cents so snipers became known as "the 13-cent killers" (though match-grade ammunition for snipers was about 20 cents).

ORGANIZATION

Key to Diagrams

Division
Regiment
Battalion
Company/battery
Platoon
Section
Squad
Infantry
Artillery
Tank
Antitank
Antitank (rocket)
Recon
Amphibian tractor
Motor transport
Machine gun
Infantry mortar
Weapons
Medical
Dental
Headquarters
Supply
Communications
Engineer
Headquarters & Service

1st Marine Division: Organization

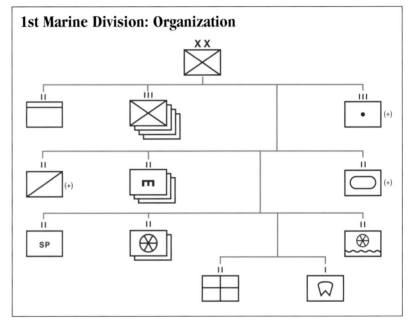

Order of Battle: 1st Marine Division, Late 1967

Headquarters Battalion

Infantry Regiments (each of 3
 battalions)
 1st Marines
 5th Marines
 7th Marines
 +27th Marines from Feb 1968

Artillery
 11th Marines (4 battalions)
 1st Field Artillery Group

1st Reconnaissance Battalion

1st Tank Battalion

1st Antitank Battalion

1st Engineer Battalion

7th Engineer Battalion

9th Engineer Battalion

3rd Amphibian Tractor Battalion

1st Motor Transport Battalion

11th Motor Transport Battalion

7th Motor Battalion

1st Shore Party Battalion

1st Medical Battalion

1st Military Police Battalion

7th Communication Battalion

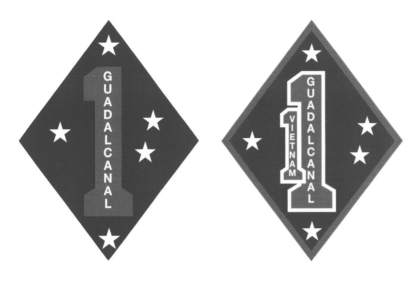

Official 1st Marine Division insignia.

Unofficial divisional insignia used in Vietnam.

11th Artillery Regiment: Organization

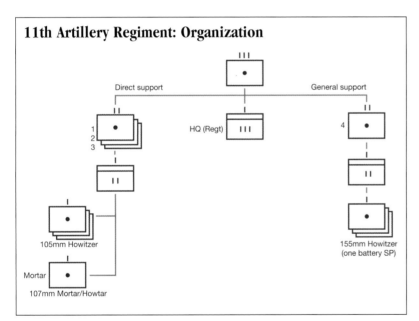

Regimental insignia, 11th Marines.

11th Artillery Regiment: Distribution of Equipment and Personnel

	HQ Btry (Regt)	HQ Btry (DS)	HQ Btry (GS)	105-mm Btry (x 9)	155-mm Btry (2 + 1)	Mortar Btry (x 3)	Total
155mm Howitzer (Towed)	–	–	–	–	6	–	12
155mm Howitzer (SP)	–	–	–	–	6	–	6
105mm Howitzer (Towed)	–	–	–	6	–	–	54
107mm Mortar/Howtar	–	–	–	–	–	6	18
USMC	218	159	157	140	122	93	2,757
USN	5	7	4	2	2	2	64

Regimental insignia, 1st Marines.

Regimental insignia, 5th Marines.

Regimental insignia, 7th Marines.

Infantry Units

Regiment

Consisted of a Headquarters Company and 3 Battalions.

Battalion

Each Battalion consisted of a Headquarters and Service Company and 4 Rifle Companies (Alpha, Bravo, Charlie, and Delta in the 1st Battalion; Echo, Foxtrot, Golf, and Hotel in the 2nd Battalion; and India, Kilo, Lima, and Mike in the 3rd Battalion). Each Headquarters and Service Company included a Communications Platoon, an M29 81-mm Mortar Platoon, a 106-mm Recoilless Rifle Platoon, Flame Thrower Section, Scout Section, Medical Section, Motor Transport Section, Supply and Support Personnel—for Operations, Intelligence, Civil Affairs, etc.

Infantry Regiment: Organization

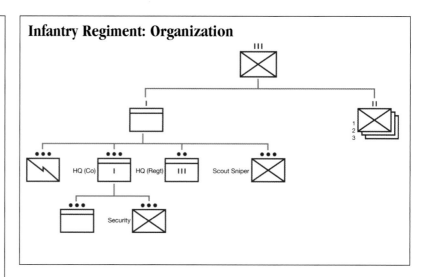

3rd Amphibian Tractor Btn: Weapons and Personnel

	H&S	HQ Plt (x2)	Amtrac Plt (x8)	Total
LVTP-5A1	12	4	10	100
LVTP-5A1 (CMD)	3	3	–	9
LVTE-1	8	–	–	8
LVTR-1A1	1	1+	–	3+
USMC	251	98	33	711
USN	15	–	–	15

Infantry Battalion: Organization

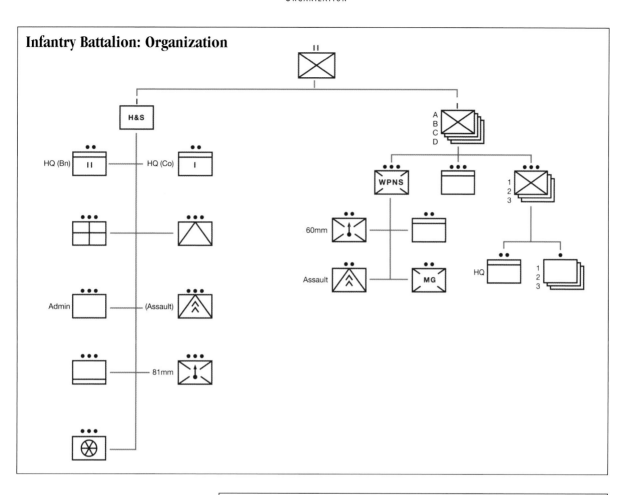

3rd Amphibian Tractor Battalion

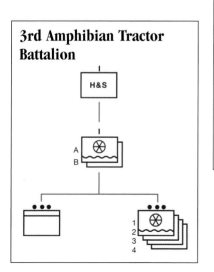

Infantry Battalion: Weapons and Personnel

	H&S Co	HQ Plt	Rifle Co Weapons Plt	Rifle Plt (x 3)	Btn Total
USMC	329	9	66	47	1,193
USN	56	–	–	–	56
M16 rifle	–	–	–	44	628
M79 grenade launcher	–	–	–	3	36
M60 machine gun	–	–	6	–	24
M19 60-mm mortar	–	–	3	–	12
M29 81-mm mortar	8	–	–	–	8
M20 3.5-in. rocket launcher	–	–	6	–	24
M40 106-mm recoilless rifle	8	–	–	–	8

1st Tank Battalion (Reinforced): Organization

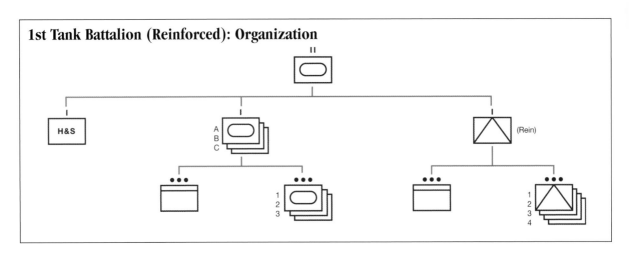

1st Tank Battalion (Reinforced): Equipment and Personnel

	H & S Co	HQ Plt (x 3)	Tank Plt (x 9)	HQ Plt (Ontos)	Ontos Plt (x 4)	Total
M48A3	–	1	5	–	–	51
M48A3 (Dozer)	–	1	–	–	–	3
M67A2 Flame Tank	9	–	–	–	–	9
M51 VTR	1	1	–	–	–	4
M50A1 Ontos	–	–	–	–	5	20
USMC	311	44	22	33	17	742
USN	15	–	–	–	–	15

Notes

Unit personnel strength shown on these pages existed on paper only. Marine units that participated in the Vietnam War were very rarely at full strength. In the infantry, it was common practice to attach the machine-gun and anti-tank elements of the weapons platoon amongst the rifle platoons within the company so that each platoon would have the firepower of two M60 Machine guns and two M20 Rocket Launchers which were often deployed against bunkers, and so on.

1st Anti-Tank Battalion: Organization

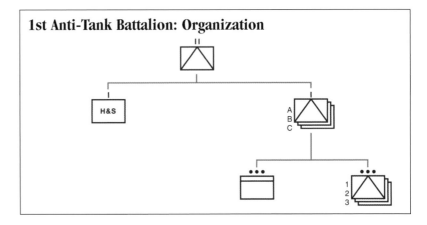

1st Anti-Tank Battalion: Equipment and Personnel

	H&S Co	HQ Plt (x 3)	Ontos Plt (x 9)	Total
M50A1 Ontos	–	–	5	45
USMC	112	15	22	355
USN	12	–	–	12

Infantry Battalion Rifle Company

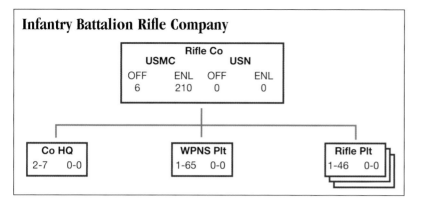

Composition of Company

1 Company HQ

3 Rifle Platoons

Each with 1 Platoon HQ,
3 Rifle Squads

1 Weapons Platoon

Weapons Platoon HQ, 1 Mortar
Squad, 1 Anti-Tank Squad, and
1 Machine Gun Squad

Company HQ

Captain

Gunnery Sergeant

1st Lieutenant (Artillery FO)

2 Corpsmen

2 Radiomen (1 for the Artillery FO)

2 Riflemen (Runners)

Rifle Platoon HQ

2nd Lieutenant

Platoon Sergeant

Right Guide

2 Corpsmen

Radioman

Rifle Squad

Sergeant (squad leader)

3 Corporals (fire team leaders)

1 Grenadier (M79)

6 Riflemen

3 Automatic Riflemen

Weapons Platoon HQ

2nd Lieutenant

Platoon Sergeant

Corpsman

2 Radiomen (one for the Mortar FO)

Mortar FO

Weapons Section (Mortar)

1 Sergeant

3 Corporals

9 Riflemen

3 M19 60-mm Mortars

Weapons Section (Anti-Tank)

1 Sergeant

3 Corporals

18 Riflemen

6 M20 3.5-inch Rocket Launchers
(later replaced by the M72 LAW)

Weapons Section (Machine Gun)

1 Sergeant

3 Corporals

18 Riflemen

6 M60 7.62-mm Machine Guns

Attached Units

At the platoon level there could be
2–5 M48 Patton tanks, 2–4 LVTP-5
Amtracs, an FO from the Battalion
Mortar Platoon and/or an FO from
the supporting Artillery Battery.
At company level, an 81-mm
section was often attached as well as
a tank platoon, an amtrac section
of 10 amtracs, an Ontos section
(2 vehicles), engineers and forward
air controllers.

The Rifle Squad

Each squad had 3 fire teams of 4
men plus a sergeant and an M79
grenadier. Each fire team had an
NCO, an automatic rifleman (with
an M14A1 rifle equipped with a
bipod for use as an automatic
weapon), and 2 riflemen. Riflemen
carried the standard M14 prior to
1967. From 1967, the Marines were
issued with the M16, though units
often retained the M14A1s for their
firepower and proven dependability.

Weapons Platoon

All troops armed with the M14/M16.

M60 Machine Gun Section

Commanded by a sergeant and
consisted of 3 M60 MG teams with 2
M60s per team. Each team had a
corporal and 2 gunners, 2 assistant
gunners, and 2 ammunition
carriers ("Ammo Humpers"). The
Marines were trained to fire the M60
using a tripod, bipod, or, if needed,
hand-held.

Anti-Tank Section

Commanded by a sergeant, and at
times referred to as the assault
section. Consisted of 3 squads. Each
had 2 weapons teams with an M20
3.5-inch Rocket Launcher, led by a
corporal, with a gunner, loader and
ammo carrier. By 1969, most M20s
had been replaced by the M72 LAW.

Mortar Section

The section was commanded by a
sergeant, with 3 squads each led by
a corporal. Each 60-mm Mortar
squad had a crew of 3 men (tube,
baseplate, and ammo). 81-mm
Mortar squads had an additional
man to carry the bipod.

PERSONALITIES

Although the Vietnam War was doomed to failure, the outcome of the conflict in no way detracted from the professionalism and abilities of the men who fought the war. In particular, the caliber of the Marine Corps commanders in Vietnam was outstanding and based on a breadth and depth of experience from many previous conflicts across the world. These embraced the tedium of protracted counterinsurgency campaigns in hostile jungle terrain from Haiti to the Dominican Republic, through the terrors of bloody fighting with the Japanese across the desolate islands of the Pacific Ocean from Guadacanal to Okinawa, and the savage battlefields of the Korean peninsula. Accordingly, they were eminently qualified to meet the challenges of the military aspects of the Vietnam conflict if given the right tools and consistent direction from Washington. In the event, these were not forthcoming and many Marines paid the ultimate price. Their lives and deaths are recorded for posterity in many publications but *Who's Who in the Marine Corps* prepared by the U.S. Marine Corps History Center is an invaluable source of information on a whole host of remarkable Marines over many generations.

Lt. Gen. Victor H. Krulak

Victor H. Krulak was born in Denver, Colorado, on 7 January 1913. Because of his diminutive stature of just 5 feet 4 inches, the height regulations had to be relaxed to allow him to attend the U.S. Naval Academy. Between studies, he became an accomplished free-style wrestler on account of which he acquired the life-long nickname of "Brute." He was commissioned as a Marine second lieutenant on 31 May 1934. His early Marine Corps service included sea duty with the Marine Detachment aboard the USS *Arizona*; an assignment at the U.S. Naval Academy and, in July 1936, duty with the 6th Marines in San Diego. He first saw active service between 1937 and 1939 in Shanghai as a company commander with the 4th Marines during the Japanese invasion of China. He was promoted to lieutenant in July 1937. In

As a young Marine Corps officer Victor Krulak enjoyed a varied and distinguished career and was instrumental in devising the equipment and doctrine for amphibious warfare at the outset of WW2.

III Marine Amphibious Force, Commanding Generals

Maj. Gen. William R. Collins	May–June 1965
Maj. Gen. Lewis W. Walt	June 1965–February 1966
Maj. Gen. Keith B. McCutcheon	February–March 1966
Lt. Gen. Lewis W. Walt	March 1966–June 1967
Lt. Gen. Robert E. Cushman	June 1967–March 1969
Lt. Gen. Herman Nickerson Jr.	March 1969–March 1970
Lt. Gen. Keith B. McCutcheon	March–December 1970
Lt. Gen. Donn J. Robertson	December 1970–April 1971

China he observed the Japanese 14-metre Daihatsu landing craft with a bow-loading ramp, an experience he used in formulating a requirement for the USMC that became the basis for the LCVP.

Lieutenant Krulak left China in May 1939 and on his return to the United States he completed the Junior Course at Marine Corps Schools, Quantico. In June 1940, he was appointed Assistant to the Brigade Quartermaster, 1st Marine Brigade, Fleet Marine Force. He was promoted to captain in August 1940. With the 1st Marine Brigade (later the 1st Marine Division), Capt. Krulak embarked for Guantanamo Bay, Cuba, in October 1940, where he was a company commander. Returning to Quantico in April 1941, he served on the staff of General Holland M. "Howling Mad" Smith, then Commanding General of Amphibious Corps, Atlantic Fleet. During this assignment he became involved in the development of the amphibian tractor to transport Marines from ship-to-shore. He organized a demonstration of a prototype vehicle for Admiral Ernest J. King, Commander-in-Chief Atlantic Fleet (later on the Joint Chiefs of Staff), who arrived in his full white dress uniform as he had a subsequent appointment with the Under-Secretary of the Navy. The admiral gave the young captain just five minutes. In that five minutes, Krulak managed to get the admiral stranded on an offshore reef with no rescue boat. Beside himself with rage, Admiral King was obliged to wade ashore in his whites and departed with the remark "Captain, have you ever considered a career as a civilian?"

Lieutenant General "Brute" Krulak and a group of officers of 9th MEB study the terrain from the top of Hill 327 west of Da Nang soon after the Marine landings in March 1965.

Medal of Honor – Captain James A. Graham was the commander of Company F, 2/5 Marines, during Operation Union II when he was killed protecting fellow wounded Marines under intense enemy fire on 2 June 1967. *See page 59.*

Medal of Honor – Lance Corporal Richard A. Pittman was a member of Company I, 3/5 Marines, during Operation Hastings when he single-handedly engaged the enemy with conspicuous gallantry on 24 July 1966 and saved the lives of many fellow Marines. *See page 32.*

The attack on Pearl Harbor intervened to forestall any abrupt career change and, in May 1942, Krulak was promoted to major. He moved with the staff of the Amphibious Corps to San Diego in September 1942 and continued as aide to the commanding general and as Assistant G-4 until January 1943, when he volunteered for parachute training. He completed training and was designated a parachutist on 15 February 1943. The following month he sailed for the Pacific and at New Caledonia took command of the 2nd Parachute Battalion, 1st Marine Amphibious Corps. He was promoted to lieutenant colonel in April 1943 and went into action that September at Vella Lavella with the 2nd New Zealand Brigade.

That October, Lt. Col. Krulak commanded the diversionary landing on Choiseul to cover the Bougainville invasion, during which action he was awarded the Navy Cross for heroism and the Purple Heart for wounds received in combat. The citation for his Navy Cross stated:

> Assigned the task of diverting hostile attention from the movements of our main attack force en route to Empress Augusta Bay, Bougainville Island, Lieutenant Colonel Krulak landed at Choiseul and daringly directed the attack of his battalion against the Japanese, destroying hundreds of tons of supplies and burning camps and landing barges. Although wounded during the assault on 30 October he repeatedly refused to relinquish his command and with dauntless courage and tenacious devotion to duty, continued to lead his battalion against the numerically superior Japanese forces.

He returned to the United States in November 1943, serving in the Division of Plans and Policies, Headquarters Marine Corps, until October 1944, when he went overseas again with the newly-formed 6th Marine Division as Assistant Chief of Staff, G-3 (Operations). Returning to the US in October 1945, Lt. Col. Krulak served at Quantico until June 1949 when he became the Regimental Commander of the 5th Marines, 1st Marine Division, at Camp Pendleton. He was promoted to colonel in August 1949. Assigned to Pearl Harbor in June 1950, Colonel Krulak was serving as Assistant Chief of Staff, G-3, Fleet Marine Force, Pacific, when the Korean conflict began. In the ensuing year, his duties took him many times to the battlefront, and during the latter half of 1951 he remained in Korea as Chief of Staff of the 1st Marine Division.

Colonel Krulak stayed in Korea until November 1951 when he returned to Washington for duty at Headquarters Marine Corps as Secretary of the General Staff, until June 1955. In August 1955, he rejoined Fleet Marine Force, Pacific, at Pearl Harbor, serving as Chief of Staff. He was promoted to brigadier general in July 1956, and assumed

1st Marine Division, Commanding Generals

Maj. Gen. Lewis J. Fields	February–October 1966
Maj. Gen. Herman Nickerson Jr.	October 1966–October 1967
Maj. Gen. Donn J. Robertson	October 1967–June 1968
Maj. Gen. Ormond R. Simpson	December 1968–December 1969
Maj. Gen. Edwin B. Wheeler	December 1969–April 1970
Maj. Gen. Charles E. Widdecke	April 1970–April 1971

Medal of Honor – Staff Sergeant Jimmie E. Howard was a member of Company C, 1st Reconnaissance Battalion, during a mission deep within enemy-dominated territory when he skilfully conducted a masterly defensive action against overwhelming enemy odds on 16 June 1966. *See page 24.*

duties as Assistant Division Commander, 3rd Marine Division, on Okinawa. On his return to the United States in July 1957, General Krulak became Director of the Marine Corps Educational Center, Quantico. While at Quantico, he was promoted to major general in November 1959. The following month, General Krulak assumed command of the Marine Corps Recruit Depot, San Diego.

In February 1962, he was appointed as the Special Assistant for Counterinsurgency and Special Activities, Organization of the Joint Chiefs of Staff. In this capacity he became highly familiar with South Vietnam and prepared comprehensive reports for President John F. Kennedy on the subject and the expanding war. General Krulak assumed command of Fleet Marine Force, Pacific, with the rank of lieutenant general, at Camp H. M. Smith, Hawaii, on 1 March 1964, For the next four years, Krulak was responsible for all Fleet Marine Force units in the Pacific, making some 54 trips to the Vietnam theater of operations. Although he had no command responsibilities on the ground, he shaped III MAF's own strategy of operations while opposing General Westmorland's fixation with "search and destroy" operations and resisting U.S. Air Force attempts to gain control of Marine airpower. Once the Marine airbase at Da Nang was established in 1965, it was decided to build another one farther south in I CTZ. The site chosen was had no name on the map so General Krulak christened the area Chu Lai, this being the characterization of Krulak's name in Mandarin, as he knew from his time in China during the 1930s.

As Commander FMF Pacific, General Krulak was accountable to Admiral Ulysses S. Grant Sharp, who as Commander-in-Chief U.S. Pacific Command (CINPAC) was responsible for the defense of an area of some 85 million square miles as well as the overall control of the war in Southeast Asia and the bombing campaign against North Vietnam. Both Krulak and Sharp were in agreement as to how to prosecute the war in Vietnam but this did not concur with the policy promulgated by Washington and the Pentagon. Both later wrote thoughtful books that make a valuable contribution to military history: *First to Fight* by Gen. Victor H. Krulak (1984) and *Strategy for Defeat: Vietnam in Retrospect* by Adm. Ulysses S. Sharp (1986).

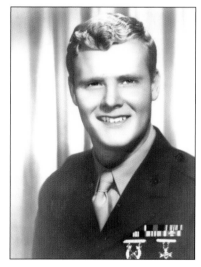

Medal of Honor – Sergeant Lawrence D. Peters was serving with Company M, 3/5 Marines, during Operation Swift when he gallantly gave his life for his country on 4 September 1967. *See page 62.*

With his sharp brain and sharp tongue, General Krulak was passed over for promotion to the post of Commandant of the U.S. Marine Corps in late 1967 and he retired on 1 June 1968.

General Krulak subsequently drew great consolation in the fact that his son, Charles C. Krulak, subsequently became the 31st Commandant of the U.S. Marine Corps.

Lt. Gen. Lewis W. Walt

Lewis William Walt was born in Wabaunsee County, Kansas, on 13 March 1913. After graduating from Colorado State University, he became a second lieutenant in the Army Field Artillery Reserve, but resigned that commission to accept an appointment as a Marine second lieutenant on 6 July 1936. In April 1937, he was assigned to the 6th Marine Regiment in San Diego as a machine-gun platoon leader. Embarking for China in August 1937, he took part in the defense of the International Settlement of Shanghai until February 1938, at which time he returned to San Diego. In June 1939, he began his second tour of overseas duty when he was assigned to the Marine Barracks in Guam. He was promoted to first lieutenant in October 1939. Returning to the United States in June 1941, Lt. Walt was assigned as a company commander in the Officer Candidates' Class, Marine Corps Schools, Quantico, Virginia. He was promoted to captain in December 1941.

Early in 1942, Captain Walt volunteered to join the 1st Marine Raider Battalion and, in April 1942, arrived with the battalion on Samoa. On 7 August 1942, as commander of Company A, 1st Raider Battalion, he landed his company in the assault on Tulagi Island in the British Solomon Islands. He was awarded the Silver Star Medal for conspicuous gallantry during the landings. Following this action, he joined the 5th Marines on Guadalcanal where he took part in combat as commander of the 2nd Battalion, 5th Marines. He was promoted to major in September 1942. In October 1942, as Battalion Commander, 2nd Battalion, 5th Marines, 1st Marine Division, Major Walt was wounded in action but continued in combat. On 22 December 1942, he was promoted in the field to lieutenant colonel for distinguished leadership and gallantry in action during the Guadalcanal campaign. In December 1943, following hospitalization and training in Australia, Lt. Col. Walt led the 2nd Battalion, 5th Marines, in the assault at Cape Gloucester, New Britain, and shortly thereafter became the Regimental Executive Officer. In the middle of this campaign he was ordered to take over command of the 3rd Battalion, 5th Marines, during the intense battle for Aogiri Ridge. In this action, he gained his first Navy Cross with Aogiri Ridge being renamed "Walt Ridge" in his honor by General Lemuel C. Shepherd, Jr, 1st Marine Division Commander.

General Walt ended his career with the U.S. Marine Corps as the Assistant Commandant as a full general and retired from duty in February 1971.

During the first half of 1944, Walt remained in the Naval Hospital, Oakland, California, for treatment of wounds and malaria. In June 1944, he returned to the Pacific area. That September, he landed at Peleliu as Regimental Executive Officer, 5th Marines. On D-day he was again ordered to take over command of the 3rd Battalion, 5th Marines, in the midst of the battle for the beachhead, when the commanding officer and executive officer were both killed. He was awarded a second Navy Cross for gallantry in this action. In November 1944, Lt. Col. Walt returned to the United States and was assigned to Marine Corps Schools, Quantico, as Chief of the Officer Candidates' School Tactics Section. In January 1947, Lt. Col. Walt became the Assistant Chief of Staff, G-3, 3rd Marine Brigade, and then G-3, 1st Marine Division. In November 1947, he assumed duty as Operations and Training Officer, 1st Provisional Marine Brigade, on Guam and later served as Chief of Staff of that organization February–April 1949. Returning to Marine Corps Schools, Quantico, in May 1949, he saw duty as a battalion commander with the Special Training Regiment, and in September he entered the Amphibious Warfare School, Senior Course. On completing the course in June 1950, he remained at Marine Corps Schools to serve as Chief of Tactics Section, S-3, and finally, Executive Officer, The Basic School. He was promoted to colonel in November 1951.

Colonel Walt was ordered to Korea in November 1952. He was in combat with the 1st Marine Division until August 1953, serving consecutively as Commanding Officer, 5th Marines, Assistant Chief of Staff, G-3, and Chief of Staff of the division. On arrival at Marine Corps Schools, Quantico, in August 1953, Col. Walt saw duty as Director, Advanced Base Problem Section, Marine Corps Educational Center, until May 1954, followed by duty as Commanding Officer, Officers' Basic School, until August 1956. He also served as a Member of the Advanced Research Group, Marine Corps Educational Center, until June 1957. Transferred to Washington, DC, Col. Walt served as Assistant Director of Personnel until August 1959, then entered the National War College. He completed the course in June 1960. In the following month, Col. Walt began a one-year assignment as Marine Corps Representative on the Joint Advanced Study Group of the Joint Chiefs of Staff. Upon completing this assignment, he was promoted to brigadier general and was appointed Assistant Division Commander, 2nd Marine Division, at Camp Lejeune. In September 1962, Gen. Walt returned to Marine Corps Schools, Quantico, serving as Director of the Marine Corps Landing Force Development Center there until May 1965. That same month, he was promoted to major general and, in June 1965, assumed command of III Marine Amphibious Force and 3rd Marine Division in South Vietnam. He was also Chief of Naval

Medal of Honor – Lieutenant Vincent R. Capodanno of the U.S. Navy Chaplain Corps was attached to 3/5 Marines during Operation Swift when he was killed assisting wounded Marines during an intense firefight on 4 September 1967. *See page 62.*

Medal of Honor – Pfc. Gary W. Martini was a member of Company F, 2/1 Marines, during Operation Union when he was killed on 21 April 1967 while attempting to save wounded Marines under extremely heavy enemy fire. *See page 55.*

Major General Lew Walt visits Marines in the field as commander of 3rd Marine Division while also serving as commander of III Marine Amphibious Force.

Lieutenant General Herman Nickerson.

Forces, Vietnam and Senior Advisor, I Corps, and I Corps Coordinator, Republic of Vietnam.

Ten months later, General Walt was nominated for lieutenant general by President Lyndon B. Johnson, and his promotion was approved by the Senate on 7 March 1966. He continued in Vietnam as Commanding General, III Marine Amphibious Force, and Senior Advisor, I Corps, and I Corps Coordinator. In accord with Gen. Kulak, he emphasized the vital necessity of pacification and the Combined Action Program as practiced by the Marine Corps in many past wars—Haiti 1915–34, Nicaragua 1926–33 or Santo Domingo 1926–33—all of which required many years of application before success was achieved. At the same time, he advocated an unfettered bombing campaign against the only strategic targets in North Vietnam: Hanoi, Haiphong, and the dikes. Only then was the war to be taken to the NVA and Main Force Viet Cong on terms favorable to American troops. This did not find favor with MACV or Washington. Such unorthodox opinions can be costly.

In late 1967, both Generals Krulak and Walt were nominated to the post of 24th Commandant of the U.S. Marine Corps. Despite their unrivalled combat experience, the appointment went to a third candidate—a Marine who had not seen combat since World War 2 and was more familiar with E-Wing than Air Wings. On 2 June 1969, General Walt was promoted to four-star rank in the post of Assistant Commandant of the Marine Corps.

General Walt retired from active duty on 1 February 1971. He died on 26 March 1989 and is buried in Quantico National Cemetery.

Lt. Gen. Herman Nickerson Jr

Herman Nickerson Jr, was born on 30 July 1913 in Boston, Massachusetts. Following graduation from Boston University, he became a Marine second lieutenant on 10 July 1935. In February 1936, Lt. Nickerson embarked for Shanghai, China, where he served for two and one-half years with the 4th Marines. On his return in November 1938, he became Commanding Officer of the Marine Detachment at the Naval Air Station, Seattle, Washington. In May 1941, he was promoted to captain while on temporary duty at the Coast Artillery School, Fort Monroe, Virginia.

Following the attack on Pearl Harbor in December 1941, Capt. Nickerson departed Parris Island for San Diego with the 2nd Defense Battalion to join the 2nd Marine Brigade overseas. Arriving on American Samoa in January 1942, he served consecutively as Battery Commander, Group Executive Officer, and finally Group Commander, 3-Inch Antiaircraft Artillery Group. While overseas, he was promoted to major in May 1942 and to lieutenant colonel in June 1943. He returned to the United States in July 1943 undertaking staff appointments until February 1945 when he again embarked for duty in the Pacific area, serving as Ordnance Officer, 4th Marine Division, and Executive Officer, 25th Marines. He later saw duty as Ordnance Officer with III Amphibious Corps in Tientsin, China, and following dissolution of III Amphibious Corps, served as Division Ordnance Officer and Division Legal Officer of the 1st Marine Division.

In January 1947, Lt. Col. Nickerson began a three-year assignment at the Marine Corps Recruit Depot, Parris Island. Following this, he completed the Armed Forces Staff College, Norfolk, Virginia, and was promoted to colonel in July 1950. In the same month, with the outbreak of hostilities in Korea, he departed for the Far East. From August 1950 to April 1951, Colonel Nickerson served as advisor on Marine Corps matters, General Headquarters, Far East Command, and also performed temporary additional duty in Korea. For conspicuous gallantry in September 1950 as Liaison Officer, 1st Marines, 1st Marine Division, during the advance along the Inchon–Seoul highway and the Han River crossing, he was awarded the Silver Star Medal. In April 1951, he took command of the 7th Marines in Korea, serving in this capacity through September 1951. During this period, he earned both the Legion of Merit with Combat "V" and subsequently, on 31 May 1951, the Army Distinguished Service Cross, the nation's second highest combat award, for extraordinary heroism. His citation stated in part:

Medal of Honor – Sergeant Alfredo Gonzalez was a member of Company A, 1/1 Marines, when he was killed at Hue City on 4 February 1968 after a series of daring attacks on enemy positions. *See pages 79–82.*

> Learning that two of his battalions were heavily engaged and that the enemy was grouping for a counter-attack, Colonel Nickerson unhesitatingly left the comparative safety of his command post and fearlessly moved forward over rugged mountainous terrain, under intense enemy mortar and artillery fire, to the most forward elements of his command. Unmindful of his personal safety, he advanced to an exposed vantage point under heavy enemy fire and through his brilliant guidance, his troops repulsed the ferocious counter-attack, taking the offensive and overwhelming the fanatical foe to secure the high ground dominating the vital road junction of Yang-gu.

Senior Marine commanders pose at Da Nang with Major General Bruno A. Hochmuth upon his arrival to assume command of 3rd Marine Division. They are, from left Major General Louis B. Robertshaw (1 MAW), Major General Herman Nickerson, Jr. (1st Marine Division), Lieutenant General Lou Walt (III MAF), General Hochmuth, and Major General Wood B. Kyle (3rd Marine Division).

Colonel Nickerson became Inspector of Fleet Marine Force, Pacific, in October 1951. In March 1952, he returned to Marine Corps Schools, Quantico, where he served as Director, Advance Base Problem Section, until June 1954, and Director, Senior School, until July 1956. He served next as Assistant Chief of Staff, G-3, Fleet Marine Force, Pacific, at Pearl Harbor, from August 1956 to December 1957. In January 1958, he joined Fleet Marine Force, Atlantic, at Norfolk, as Assistant Chief of Staff, G-3. Transferred to Headquarters Marine Corps in September 1958, Colonel Nickerson served as Special Assistant to the Fiscal Director until April 1959, when he was named Fiscal Director of the Marine Corps. He was promoted to brigadier general on 1 January 1959. In June 1962, he assumed command of the 1st Marine Division at Camp Pendleton. He was promoted to major general on 1 July 1962.

In April 1963, General Nickerson joined the Marine Corps Supply Center, Barstow, California, as Commanding General. He served as Commanding General, Marine Corps Base, Camp Lejeune, North Carolina, from June 1965 until September 1966. In October 1966, General Nickerson assumed command of the 1st Marine Division in South Vietnam until May 1967, earning the Distinguished Service Medal for this and his subsequent service as Deputy Commander, III Marine Amphibious Force from June 1967 to October 1967.

Upon his return to the United States in November 1967, he served briefly as Assistant Chief of Staff, G-3, at Headquarters Marine Corps. In January 1968, he was assigned duty as Director of Personnel/Deputy Chief of Staff (Manpower), and shortly after was nominated for lieutenant general by President Johnson and his promotion confirmed by the Senate, 15 March 1968. One year later, in March 1969, he returned to Vietnam as Commanding General, III Marine Amphibious Force.

General Nickerson retired after 35 years as a Marine on 31 March 1970. He died on 27 December 2000 in Maine.

ASSESSMENT

The Vietnam War remains contentious to this day. The U.S. armed forces won virtually every encounter with the enemy on the ground, in the air, and at sea but they lost the war. America's war aims were primarily to prevent the communist takeover of South Vietnam, set within the context of the wider Cold War. The war aims of Hanoi were to unite North and South Vietnam at any cost. In April 1975, South Vietnam was defeated by a conventional military invasion from the North. The neighboring countries of Cambodia and Laos soon fell victim to the communists. Conflict continued to rage across Southeast Asia during the 1970s and early 1980s as the various communist factions fought each other for dominance. Throughout this period, the United States turned its back on this region of the world that had caused so much trauma. Many questions remained unresolved. The most fundamental of all was whether the war was ever winnable at all given the military strategy adopted by MACV as against that proposed by the U.S. Marine Corps. From the outset, the commanders of III MAF and Fleet Marine Force, Pacific, were at variance with General Westmoreland and MACV over the conduct of the war. With long experience in counterinsurgency campaigns in the Philippines and the "Banana Wars" in Latin America, the Marine Corps had very clear ideas on how to prosecute the war in Vietnam.

With a traditional Marine "Devil Dog" tattoo on his bicep, a squad leader orders his men of 1/7 Marines to move forward on the first day of Operation Stockton on 27 July 1967. Note the double dogtags around the neck and the lack of camouflaged helmet cover which was unusual in the Marines.

These were encapsulated in *The Small Wars Manual*, published in 1940, that was a synthesis of USMC warfighting skills and experience over the previous 150 years of conflict across the globe; most of this was to protect civilian populations from armed insurrection. Fundamental to this was pacification and the need to separate the innocent civilian population from the malign influence and depredations of the insurgents. The key to this was the "inkblot strategy" whereby U.S. forces would gradually enlarge and consolidate their coastal enclaves until they embraced the bulk of the civil population who lived predominately in the coastal regions where rice grew in abundance. Only once their security had been achieved, should allied forces then

With the legend NO NAME emblazoned on the gun barrel, an M48A3 (Model B) engages the treeline as Marines on the rear engine decks shelter their ears from the blast. Within the Marine Corps ethos, the primary role of any weapon system was to support the Marine combat rifleman. The hydraulic pipes on the rear fender indicate that this is a dozer tank.

search out and destroy the insurgents in the hinterland. As General "Brute" Krulak graphically stated: "The conflict between the North Vietnamese and hard-core Viet Cong, on the one hand, and the U.S. on the other, could move to another planet today and we would not have won the war. On the other hand, if the subversion and guerrilla efforts were to disappear, the war would soon collapse, as the enemy would be denied food, sanctuary and intelligence."

At the same time, General Krulak and III MAF were keen to strike North Vietnam hard at the only important military and industrial targets that were vulnerable to strategic bombing—the Red River dikes, the road and rail links with China, Hanoi, and the comprehensive mining of Haiphong harbour where the bulk of the communist war materiel arrived from the Soviet Union and Eastern Europe. These were the specific target areas denied to the U.S Air Force and U.S. Navy by Washington in the time frame that really mattered—1965 and 1966. The overriding fear in Washington was that bombing Hanoi and Haiphong would provoke a Chinese intervention into the war as occurred in Korea. But China was still convulsed by the Great Leap Forward and then the Cultural Revolution. It was in no fit state to intervene. Indeed, it did not do so after the U.S. Air Force and U.S. Navy did eventually strike these targets in 1972. But by then it was too little, too late. Instead, Washington pursued a misguided policy of "graduated response" with Operation Rolling Thunder to try and force the North Vietnamese to the conference table through the application of airpower. Based on a largely agrarian society, North Vietnam's war effort was barely damaged by the bombing campaign and its main result was to unite the people behind the communist regime. Furthermore it cost the American taxpayer $10 for every $1 of damage inflicted on the North Vietnamese economy, let alone the cost in destroyed aircraft and lost aircrews. U.S. airpower dropped 800 tons of bombs a day on North Vietnam for three and a half years while the import of war materiel through Haiphong more than doubled in the same period. As Henry Kissinger wryly observed—the bombing campaign was "powerful enough to mobilize world opinion against us but too half-hearted and gradual to be decisive." On occasions, President Johnson instituted bombing pauses as a goodwill gesture but Hanoi saw them as a sign of weakness. Invariably the communists took the opportunity to reinforce their air-defense systems, which eventually became among the most extensive in the world.

Marines of Company F, 2/7 Marines, board an LCM (Landing Craft Medium) on 30 November 1967 at the conclusion of Operation Foster/Badger Hunt conducted in the "Da Nang rocket belt" with Badger Hunt being the SLF element of the operation.

Burdened down with an M19 60-mm mortar, a Marine of 2/5 Marines wades across a stream during a patrol near An Hoa Combat Base on 10 August 1967. With an effective range of up to 2,000 yards, the M19 provided the quickest fire support within the rifle company, although its weight often proved an excessive burden in the field. The 60-mm mortar could also be used without the M2 Mortar Bipod as a handheld weapon. This made it considerably easier to carry at just 12.8 pounds as against 42.5 pounds fully assembled with bipod and baseplate.

This reveals some of the complexities of the Vietnam War which in fact was several wars being fought at once. These included the Cold War itself against the expansion of communism and, within that, the political war between Washington and Hanoi in their continuing quest to win over world opinion; the "hearts and minds" campaign to gain the allegiance of the South Vietnamese people through pacification; the gruelling ground war against the NVA and VC; the bombing offensive against the North and the Ho Chi Minh Trail; and, last but not least, the vital necessity to maintain the support of the American people for the war and its purpose. Of these, the most important was pacification as advocated by the USMC. The "Marine inkblot strategy" was considered at the highest levels of the military and political establishments, including Chairman of the Joint Chiefs of Staff, General Harold K. Johnson, and Secretary for Defense, Robert S. McNamara, but was rejected in December 1965. General Krulak recalled:

> Many people applauded the idea, among them Army Generals Maxwell Taylor and James Gavin. General Westmoreland told me, however, that while the inkblot idea seemed to be effective, we just didn't have time to do it that way. I suggested to him that we didn't have time to do it any other way; if we left the people to the enemy, glorious victories in the hinterland would be little more than blows in the air and we would end up losing the war.

And that is exactly what happened.

Even if the Marine strategy had been fully adopted it would have taken decades of concerted military and pacification efforts to succeed and only then with a radical overhaul of the political regime in Saigon; until comprehensive land reform was introduced to allow the peasants to own their own property South Vietnam could never function as a proper democratic country. Even then the problems would have been insurmountable as there could be no real security if the political establishment allowed the enemy to build and maintain secure sanctuaries with impunity along South Vietnam's long and ill-defined borders in its so-called neutral neighboring countries. For the Marines in I CTZ, the enemy held a particular advantage with safe sanctuaries nearby in both North Vietnam and Laos with many infiltration routes into the region. Denied the military option to root out these base camps, III MAF was hamstrung from the outset, as was MACV. Furthermore, it must be questioned whether the Marines should have been in I CTZ at all.

The U.S. Marine Corps is first and foremost an amphibious assault force. Accordingly its whole structure is predicated on being self-contained and supplied by sea. The Marine Corps ethos was and

remains centered on the combat rifleman and what he can carry into battle. It is all the more curious then that what was essentially a light-infantry force should be deployed to the one area of South Vietnam where a conventional invasion by the North Vietnamese Army was expected to occur by MACV. Tied to defensive positions along the DMZ and the ineffectual McNamara Line, the Marine Corps was denied its true calling of amphibious warfare. It would have seemed logical to have employed the Marines in the one area of South Vietnam where that expertise could have been truly effective: in the innumerable waterways and inundated areas of the Mekong Delta and the Rung Sat Special Zone of the Saigon River estuary that were of such fundamental strategic importance. Instead the vital IV CTZ region was left as a virtual ARVN fiefdom and, even more curiously, MACV decided to convert the 2nd Brigade of the hastily formed U.S. Army 9th Infantry Division into an amphibious force supported by the U.S. Navy and, often, by the Vietnamese Marine Corps, which was trained, of course, by the USMC.

Inter-service rivalry is inevitable and often healthy in maintaining a competitive edge within the armed forces but in Vietnam it became another serious aggravation in the failure of the overall military

"Get Some Charlie!"—riflemen of 2nd Platoon, Company L, 3/5 Marines, return fire during Operation Meade River in the Dodge City area southwest of Da Nang on 30 November 1968. Typically each rifleman carried 50-round linked belts of 7.62-mm ammunition to serve the squad M60 machine gun. To serve his own weapon, this rifleman has a cotton bandoleer across his chest for ready access to seven 20-round M16 magazines.

Lance Corporal Ernest J. Antol of Company C, 1st Engineer Battalion, attached to Company M, 3/7 Marines, struggles through the glutinous mud of a paddy field near the hamlet of Chau Son II on 20 November 1968. Although a combat engineer, he is also a Marine rifleman, as his M16 rifle and ammunition bandoleer attest. He carries the tools of his trade in a "demolitions bag" slung over his shoulder, probably including blocks of C-4 explosive and detonation cord. One of the main missions of the combat engineer in the field was the clearing of mines and neutralization of booby-traps as well as destroying any unexploded US ordnance that the enemy might use for their own purposes.

strategy. The largely irrelevant strategic bombing campaign absorbed enormous resources that could have been better utilized elsewhere. The conventional-warfare doctrine pursued by MACV and the Pentagon was also hugely expensive and massively destructive to the infrastructure of South Vietnam; more bombs were dropped on this allied country than on all the Axis powers in World War 2. As in the Korean War before, it is difficult to understand why the Marine Corps was so misused by the U.S. Army and MACV in South Vietnam by being deployed in I CTZ. But then it is just as difficult to understand why the Marine Corps has been deployed more recently in Anbar Province in Iraq, as far from the sea as it is possible to be in that benighted country.

In Korea, in South Vietnam and in Iraq, the U.S. Marine Corps has been systematically misemployed as a standard infantry formation, compromising its true operational rationale. It is as if the U.S. Army wishes to deny a rival of its purpose and by extension its existence, like the NVA achieved of the NLF in the Tet Offensive.

The National Security Act of 1947 defined the three primary roles of the U.S. Marine Corps as follows:

1. The seizure or defense of advanced naval bases and other land operations to support naval campaigns.
2. The development of tactics, techniques and equipment used by amphibious landing forces.
3. Such other duties as the President may direct.

Sheltering in their foxholes, men of the 3rd Platoon, Mike Company, 3/7 Marines, stand ready in defense of Sa Binh village against a possible Viet Cong attack during Operation Desoto. Note the M40 rounds lying readily to hand beside the M79 grenadier in the background.

The first is quite specific and emphasizes the USMC attachment to the U.S. Navy and the Navy Department over the U.S. Army. The second is equally specific. It is manifested in such new weapon systems as the revolutionary tilt-rotor V-22 Osprey, the LCAC (Landing Craft Air Cushion) and the Expeditionary Fighting Vehicle, the latest in a long line of amtracs. These will give the Marine Corps much-enhanced landing capabilities both by air and by sea. What remains in question is the concept of amphibious warfare itself in this modern age when the last contested landing conducted by the USMC happened in 1950 during the Korean War. Just as with airborne paratroop operations, the doctrine of amphibious warfare risks becoming an expensive anachronism on the modern battlefield. Accordingly, the U.S. Marine Corps is at the forefront of a new war-fighting doctrine for the 21st century known as "Distributed Operations" that owes much to the "small wars" concept of yore. Operating from secure sea bases, it gives far greater autonomy for small-unit actions in a world of increasingly complex geopolitical problems.

It is in the third role that the Marine Corps excels and remains the elite within the U.S. armed forces. No other arm of service allows the President of the United States such flexibility to react to crises and situations across the world. With Marine expeditionary units afloat

This classic image of grunts in the field graphically illustrates the burden they carried on operations, particularly an M60 team as shown here. Lance Cpl. Larry W. Elam is laden down with his M60 across his shoulders under a rain cover and a whole host of equipment. He and his assistant gunner, Pfc. R. S. Gonzales, are carrying a C-Ration carton and an ammunition box containing 200 rounds. Elam is wearing the camouflage tropical combat uniform first issued in late 1968 and classified Coat/Trousers, Man's, Camouflage Cotton, Wind Resistant Poplin, Class 2. Over this he has his M1955 fragmentation vest and on his back an M1941 haversack with a rolled rain poncho and a half-deflated "rubber bitch" air mattress attached to the outside.

across the seven seas, the Marine Corps acts as the primary instrument of American power projection able to intervene on land in virtually any country where American interests are threatened. With its integral naval and tactical air support, any Marine landing force can now be readily enhanced by Air Force strategic aircraft, both bombers and transports, flying directly from the United States. With the specter of nuclear warfare between opposing superpowers now diminished, it is all the more important to have the capability to undertake amphibious and airborne landings across the globe for both military and humanitarian purposes, be it Somalia or Rwanda.

This capability has been compromised by prolonged commitments to land campaigns such as those in Korea, Vietnam and Iraq; both the Korean and Vietnam Wars caused considerable institutional damage that required years to rectify. Yet, to the Marines themselves, they have always followed their Presidents' call to arms be it in the Philippine Insurrection or the Boxer Rebellion in China, in the "Banana Wars" of Latin America or at Belleau Wood, in the Pacific islands or the mudflats of Inchon, and in the killing fields of Vietnam from "Leatherneck Square" to the "Arizona Territory." On each and every occasion, the Marines undertook their duty to the best of their abilities living up to their motto *Semper Fidelis*—"Always Faithful."

Introduced in 1960, the M60 General Purpose Machine Gun replaced the classic Browning M1919 machine gun and BAR—Browning Automatic Rifle—of World War 2 fame as the standard infantry automatic weapon. Here, Marines of Bravo Company, 1/7 Marines, return fire during a firefight on 22 May 1970.

REFERENCE

Cricital Biblography

The Marine Corps in Vietnam, Charles Melson (Osprey, Oxford, 1998). This volume is an excellent primer on the USMC in Vietnam covering the basic background to the war; enlistment and training; uniforms and weapons and everyday life as well as some combat actions in Vietnam as seen through the eyes of some notional Marines of the 9th Regiment of 3rd Marine Division. As always Osprey provides some excellent colour plates to illustrate typical Marine weapons and equipment.

Vietnam: U.S. Uniforms in Colour Photographs, Kevin Lyles (Windrow & Greene, London, 1992). There are many books on the uniforms and equipment of U.S. forces in Vietnam but this book gives a thorough grounding in the subject through numerous reconstructions of various soldiers and Marines depicted throughout the campaign with full descriptions of clothing, personal equipment and the wide diversity of weapons used in combat.

The US Marine Corps in the Vietnam War: III Marine Amphibious Force 1965–75, Ed Gilbert (Osprey, Oxford, 2006). Written by a Marine Vietnam Veteran, this volume in the Osprey Battle Orders series details the complete organization of III Marine Amphibious Force covering doctrine and training; unit organization; logisitics; and weapons together with the overall strategy and tactics employed on combat operations. Profusely illustrated the book also provides numerous diagrams of unit organization and equipment in a clear and precise manner.

The Story of the U.S. Marine Corps, J. Robert Moskin (Paddington Press, New York & London 1979). Vietnam was but one campaign in the illustrious history of the US Marine Corps. This book provides a comprehensive and highly readable record of the Corps from its inception up to the aftermath of Vietnam in a single volume.

This volume is an excellent concise reference to the uniforms and personal equipment of military personnel during the Vietnam War.

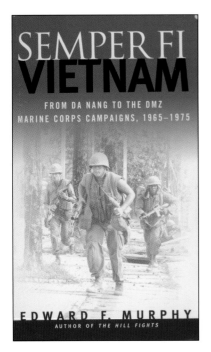

ABOVE: *Semper Fi Vietnam* is an outstanding single-volume history of the USMC during the Vietnam War that is available in softback.

The Marines in Vietnam, 1954–1973, HQ U.S. Marine Corps (1974). This book was the first of many written about the campaign by the USMC History and Museums Division in Washington DC. Drawing on articles published previously in the *US Marine Corps Gazette* and *Leatherneck* magazines, this volume has an immediacy and a wealth of information despite its basic design and dated typography.

Also published by the USMC History and Museums Division are the Marine Corps Vietnam Series Operational Histories. These books are essential reading for any serious student interested in the military history of the U.S. Marine Corps during the protracted Vietnam War.

U.S. Marines in Vietnam: 1954–1964, The Advisory and Combat Assistance Era (1977)
U.S. Marines in Vietnam: 1965, The Landing and the Buildup (1978)
U.S. Marines in Vietnam: 1966, An Expanding War (1982)
U.S. Marines in Vietnam: 1967, Fighting the North Vietnamese (1984)
U.S. Marines in Vietnam: 1968, The Defining Year (1997)
U.S. Marines in Vietnam: 1969, High Mobility and Standdown (1988)
U.S. Marines in Vietnam: 1970–1971, Vietnamization and Redeployment (1986)
U.S. Marines in Vietnam: 1971–1973, The War that Would Not End (1991
U.S. Marines in Vietnam: 1973–1975, The Bitter End (1990)

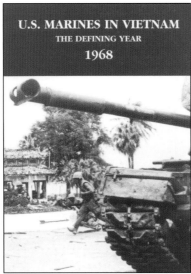

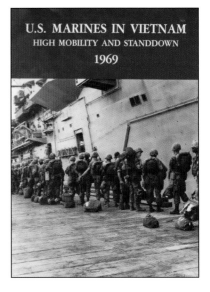

ABOVE: Examples from the Operational Histories series.

All these volumes are well illustrated with photographs incorporating informative captions. They are available in print at the cost of just a few dollars from the outlets listed below as well as online as free of charge downloadable pdfs.

Another useful publication from the History Division is *Small Unit Action in Vietnam*, F. J. West (Washington DC, 1967) as is his later book *The Village* published by Harper and Row, New York, 1972.

Websites

The official website of the USMC History Division can be found at <http://hqinet001.hqmc.usmc.mil/HD>. This allows access to the Historical Branch and the Historical Reference Branch together with the numerous publications released by the USMC on the Vietnam War and other campaigns over the years. The official website <http://www.i-mef.usmc.mil/DIV> takes one to the home page of the 1st Marine Division which provides a wealth of information from the telephone number of the commanding general to current activities of the division around the world.

The websites of the two official USMC magazines—*US Marine Corps Gazette* and *Leatherneck are:* <http://www.mca-marines.org/gazette> and <http://www.mca-marines.org/leatherneck>. These can now be accessed online.

Museum

The **National Museum of the Marine Corps** opened on 13 November 2006 and is located at 18900 Jefferson Davis Hwy., Triangle, VA 22172; email: <info@usmcmuseum.org>. This magnificent museum is the centerpiece of The Marine Corps Heritage Center set in a 135-acre site incorporating the Semper Fidelis Memorial Park and Chapel. The museum has absorbed the artifacts of the Marine Corps Air-Ground Museum, formerly based at Quantico. Many of the books mentioned above are available from the Museum: <http://www.marineheritage.org/Store_index.asp>.

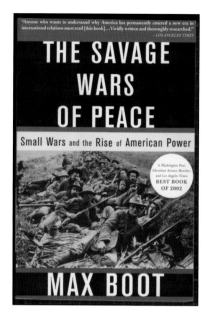

ABOVE: Max Boot is an award-winning historian. His book *The Savage Wars of Peace* is essential reading for any student of military history wishing to understand the ethos and lineage of the USMC and the concept of "Small Wars."

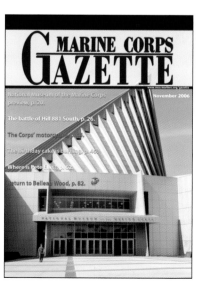

SECOND LEFT: The website of the Marine Corps Heritage Foundation is itself an excellent source of information as well as providing links to other sites of interest.

LEFT: The *Marine Corps Gazette* includes articles on many aspects of Marine history and current events. This recent edition also featured coverage of the National Museum.

INDEX